ENCYCLOPAEDIC DICTIONARY OF INTERNATIONAL BUSINESS MANAGEMENT

ENCYCLOPAEDIC DICTIONARY OF INTERNATIONAL BUSINESS MANAGEMENT

Vol. 1

by

A.S. SUDAN

ANMOL PUBLICATIONS PVT. LTD.

NEW DELHI-110 002 (INDIA)

ANMOL PUBLICATIONS PVT. LTD.
4374/4B, Ansari Road, Daryaganj
New Delhi-110 002
Phones: 23261597, 23278000, 23255577
Email: anmolpublications@vsnl.com

Encyclopaedic Dictionary of International Business Management

First Edition 2003
ISBN 81-261-1508-4 (Set)

PRINTED IN INDIA

Published by J.L. Kumar for Anmol Publications Pvt. Ltd., New Delhi-110 002 and Printed at Mehra Offset Press, Delhi.

PREFACE

Conventionally, 'Business' is understood as a trade or profession; an industrial, commercial, or professional operation; purchase and sale of goods and services; a commercial or industrial establishment; commercial activity; volume or quantity of commercial activity; commercial policy or procedure etc. Business operations are mainly divided into—technical, commercial, financial, security, accounting and managerial activities. Till recently managerial skills had been most neglected aspect of business operations. The term 'managing' consists of various functions, main among which are—planning, organising, commanding, coordinating and controlling.

Amidst the various schools of management thought Business Management can rightly considered as an art, a science and a profession.

As is obvious from the name of the title, the present work contains judiciously selected and well explained terms covering the International Business Management in entirety. This encyclopaedic dictionary will prove a reliable asset to one and all in the field.

—A.S. Sudan

A

Fifth letter of a Nasdaq stock symbol specifying Class A shares.

AAA+ Bank

Banks are rated according to their credit worthiness by IBCA, Moodys investor service and Standard & Poors. The only AAA bank in the US is JP Morgan.

AAII

See: American Association of Individual Investors.

Abandonment

Controlling party giving up rights to property voluntarily.

Abandonment option

The option of terminating an investment earlier than originally planned.

ABC agreement

A contract between an employee and a brokerage firm outlining the rights of the firm purchasing an NYSE membership for that employee.

Ability to pay

Refers to the borrower's ability to make interest and principal payments on debts. See: Fixed charge coverage ratio. In context of municipal bonds, refers to the issuer's present and future ability to create sufficient tax revenue to fulfill its contractual obligations, accounting for municipal income and property values. In context of taxation, notion that tax rates should be determined according to income or wealth.

Abnormal returns

The component of the return that is not due to systematic influences (market-wide influences). In other words, abnormal returns are above those predicted by the market movement alone. Related: excess returns.

ABO

See: Accumulated Benefit Obligation.

Above par

See: Par.

ABS

See: Automated Bond System.

Absolute advantage

A person, company or country has an absolute advantage if its output per unit of input of all goods and services produced is higher than that of another person, company or country.

Absolute form of purchasing power parity

A theory that prices of products of two different countries should be equal when measured by a common currency. Also called the "law of one price."

Absolute Physical Life

The period of use after which an asset has deteriorated to such an extent that it can no longer be used.

Absolute Priority

Rule in bankruptcy proceedings requiring senior creditors to be paid in full before junior creditors receive any payment.

Absorbed

Used in context of general equities. Securities are "absorbed" as long as there are corresponding orders to buy and sell. The market has reached the absorption point when further assimilation is impossible without an adjustment in price. See: Sell the book.

Absorption

Absorption is investment and consumption purchases by households, businesses, and governments, both domestic and imported. When absorption exceeds production, the excess is the country's current account deficit.

Abu Dhabi Fund for Arab Economic Development (ADFAED)

ADFAED promotes economic and social development in African, Arab, and Asian developing countries. The Fund, which was created in July 1971, began operations in September 1974; headquarters are in Abu Dhabi, United Arab Emirates.

Abusive tax shelter

A limited partnership that the IRS judges to be claiming tax deductions illegally.

ACAT

See: Automated Customer Account Transfer.

Accelerated Cost Recovery System (ACRS)

Schedule of depreciation rates allowed for tax purposes.

Acceleration clause

A contract stating that the unpaid balance becomes due and payable if specific actions transpire, such as failure to make interests payments on time.

Accelerated depreciation

Any depreciation method that produces larger deductions for depreciation in the early years of a asset's life. Accelerated cost recovery system (ACRS), which is a depreciation schedule allowed for tax purposes, is one such example.

Acceptance

This term has several related meanings:

1. A time draft (or bill of exchange) which the drawee has accepted and is unconditionally obligated to pay at maturity. The draft must be presented first for acceptance - the drawee becomes the "acceptor" and the date and place of payment must be written on the face of the draft.
2. The drawee's act in receiving a draft and thus entering into the obligation to pay its value at maturity.
3. Any agreement to purchase goods under specified terms. An agreement to purchase goods at a stated price and under stated terms.

Accession

Accession is the process by which a country becomes a member of an international agreement, such as the General Agreement on Tariffs and Trade (GATT) or the European Community. Accession to the GATT involves negotiations to determine the specific obligations a nonmember country must undertake before it will be entitled to full GATT membership benefits.

Accommodative monetary policy

Federal Reserve System policy to increase the amount of money available to banks for lending. See: Monetary policy.

Accord

See International Agreements.

Account

In the context of bookkeeping, refers to the ledger pages upon which various assets, liabilities, income, and expenses are represented.

In the context of investment banking, refers to the status of securities sold and owned or the relationship between parties to an underwriting syndicate. In the context of securities, the relationship between a client and a broker/dealer firm allowing the firm's employee to be the client's buying and selling agent. See: Account executive; account statement.

Account Ad Valorem Duty

An imported merchandise tax expressed as a percentage.

Account balance

Credits minus debits at the end of a reporting period.

Account executive

The brokerage firm employee who handles stock orders for clients. See: Broker.

Account Party

The buyer under a letter of credit. The party ultimately responsible for reimbursing the issuing bank for all payments extended on its behalf.

Account reconciliation

The reviewing and adjusting of the balance in a personal checkbook to match your bank statement.

Account statement

In the context of banking, refers to a summary of all balances.

In the context of securities, a summary of all transactions and positions (long and short) between a broker/dealer and a client. See also: Option agreement.

Accountant's opinion

A signed statement from an independent public accountant after examination of a firm's records and accounts. The opinion may be unqualified or qualified. See: Qualified opinion.

Accounting earnings

Earnings of a firm as reported on its income statement.

Accounting exposure

The change in the value of a firm's foreign currency-denominated accounts due to a change in exchange rates.

Accounting insolvency

Total liabilities exceed total assets. A firm with a negative net worth is insolvent on the books.

Accounting liquidity

The ease and quickness with which assets can be converted to cash.

Accounts payable

Money owed to suppliers.

Accounts receivable

Money owed by customers.

Accounts receivable financing

A short-term financing method in which accounts receivable are collateral for cash advances. See: Factoring.

Accounts receivable turnover

The ratio of net credit sales to average accounts receivable, which is a measure of how quickly customers pay their bills.

Accredited investor

Refers to an individual whose net worth, or joint net worth with a spouse, exceeds $1,000,000; or whose individual income exceeded $200,000 or whose joint income with a spouse exceeded $300,000 in each of the 2 most recent years and can be expected to meet that income in the current year. More details of the definitions for investors other that individuals are found in Regulation D of the Securities and Exchange Commission.

Accretion (of a discount)

In portfolio accounting, a straight-line accumulation of capital gains on a discount bond in anticipation of receipt of par at maturity.

Accrual Accounting Convention

An accounting system that tries to match the recognition of revenues earned with the expenses incurred in generating those revenues. It ignores the timing of the cash flows associated with revenues and expenses.

Accrual basis

In the context of accounting, practice in which expenses and income are accounted for as if they are earned or incurred, whether or not they have been received or paid. Antithesis of cash basis accounting.

Accrual bond

A bond on which interest accrues but is not paid to the investor during the time of accrual. The amount of accrued interest is added to the remaining principal of the bond and is paid at maturity.

Accrued benefits

The pension benefits earned by an employee accourding to the years of the employee's service.

Accrued discount

Interest that accumulates on savings bonds from the date of purchase until the date of redemption or final maturity, whichever comes first. Series A, B, C, D, E, EE, F, I, and J are discount or accrual bonds, meaning principal and interest are paid when the bonds are redeemed. Series G, H, HH, and K are current-income bonds, and the semiannual interest paid to their holders is not included in accrued discount.

Accrued interest

Applies mainly to convertible securities. Interest that has accumulated between the most recent payment and the sale of a bond or other fixed-income security. At the time of sale, the buyer pays the seller the bond's price plus "accrued interest," calculated by multiplying the coupon rate by the fraction of the coupon period that has elapsed since the last payment.

(If a bondholder receives $40 in coupon payments per bond semiannually and sells the bond one-quarter of the way into the coupon period, the buyer pays the seller $10 as the latter's proportion of interest earned.)

Accrued market discount

The rise in the market value of a discount bond as it approaches maturity (when it is redeemable at par) and not because of falling market interest rates.

Accumulate

Broker/analyst recommendation that could mean slightly different things depending on the broker/analyst. In general, it means to increase the number of shares of a particular security over the near term, but not to liquidate other parts of the portfolio to buy a security that might skyrocket. A buy recommendation, but not an urgent buy.

Accumulated Benefit Obligation (ABO)

An approximate measure of the liability of a pension plan in the event of a termination at the date the calculation is performed. Related: Projected benefit obligation.

Accumulated dividend

A dividend that has reached its due date, but is not paid out. See: Cumulative preferred stock.

Accumulated profits tax

A tax on earnings kept in a firm to prevent the higher personal income tax rate that would obtain if profits were paid out as dividends to the owners.

Accumulation

In the context of corporate finance, refers to profits that are added to the capital base of the company rather than paid out as dividends. See: Accumulated profits tax. In the context of investments, refers to the purchase by an institutional broker of a large number of shares over a period of time in order to avoid pushing the price of that share up. In the context of mutual funds, refers to the regular investing of a fixed amount while reinvesting dividends and capital gains.

Accumulation area

A price range within which a buyer accumulates shares of a stock. See: On-balance volume and distribution area.

ACES

See: Advance Computerized Execution System.

ACH

See: Automated Clearing House.

Acid test ratio

Also called the quick ratio, the ratio of current assets minus inventories, accruals, and prepaid items to current liabilities.

Acknowledgement

A form used by a vendor to advise a purchaser that his/her order has been received, and usually to imply that it has been accepted.

Acquired surplus

The surplus acquired when a company is purchased in a pooling of interests combination, i.e. the net worth not considered to be capital stock.

Acquiree

A firm that is being acquired.

Acquirer

A firm or individual that is acquiring something.

Acquisition

Subject to national and local laws and regulations a company may acquire and hold the shares of stock and other securities of one or more other corporations and businesses. Acquired companies may continue operating as independent organizations with their own names and personnel.

Acquisition cost

Refers to the price (including the closing costs) to purchase another company or property.

In the context of investments, refers to price plus brokerage commissions, of a security, or the sales charge applied to load funds. See: Tax basis.

Acquisition of assets

A merger or consolidation in which an acquirer purchases the selling firm's assets.

Acquisition of stock

A merger or consolidation in which an acquirer purchases the acquiree's stock.

Across the board

Movement or trend in the stock market that affects almost all stocks in all sectors to move in the same direction.

ACRS

See: Accelerated cost recovery system.

Acting in concert

Investors working together and performing identical actions to attain the same investment goal.

Act of God

A natural event, not preventable by any human agency, such as flood, storms, or lightning. Forces of nature that a carrier has no control over, and therefore cannot be held accountable.

Act of state doctrine

This doctrine says that a nation is sovereign within its own borders, and its domestic actions may not be questioned in the courts of another nation.

Active

A market in which there is frequent trading.

Active account

Refers to a brokerage account in which many transactions occur. Brokerage firms may levy a fee if an account generates an inadequate level of activity.

Active bond crowd

Refers to members of the bond department of the NYSE who trade the most bonds. Antithesis of cabinet crowd.

Active box

Securities that are held in safekeeping and are available as collateral for securing brokers' loans or customers' margin positions.

Active fund management

An investment approach that purposely shifts funds either between asset classes (asset allocation) or between individual securities (security selection).

Active income

Income from an active business as opposed to passive investment income according to the U.S. tax code.

Active Management

The pursuit of investment returns in excess of a specified benchmark.

Active portfolio strategy

A strategy that uses available information and forecasting techniques to seek better performance than a buy and hold portfolio. Related: Passive portfolio strategy.

Active Return

Return relative to a benchmark. If a portfolio's return is 5%, and the benchmark's return is 3%, then the portfolio's active return is 2%.

Active Risk

The risk (annualized standard deviation) of the active return. Also called the tracking error.

Actual market

Used in context of general equities. Firm market. Antithesis of Subject market.

Actuals

The physical commodities underlying a futures contract. Cash commodity, physical asset.

ACU

See: Asian currency units.

AD

The two-character ISO 3166 country code for ANDORRA.

A-D

Advance-Decline, or measurement of the number of issues trading above their previous closing prices less the number trading below their previous closing prices over a particular period. As a technical measure of market breadth, the steepness of the AD line indicates whether a strong bull or bear market is under way.

ADB

See: Adjusted Debit Balance.

Additional bonds test

A test for ensuring that bond issuers can meet the debt service requirements of issuing any new additional bonds.

Additional hedge

A protection against borrower fallout risk in the mortgage pipeline.

Additionality

Clause in a countertrade contract prescribing that a primary supplier's countertrade obligation can be fulfilled only by incremental exports above achieved trade levels to traditional markets, or by exports to new markets.

Adequacy of coverage

A test that measures the extent to which the value of an asset is protected from potential loss either through insurance or hedging.

ADFAED

See Abu Dhabi Fund for Arab Economic Development.

Adjustable rate

Applies mainly to convertible securities. Refers to interest rate or dividend that is adjusted periodically, usually according to a standard market rate outside the control of the bank or savings institution, such as that prevailing on Treasury bonds or notes. Typically, such issues have a set floor or ceiling, called caps and collars that limits the adjustment.

Adjustable-rate mortgage (ARM)

A mortgage that features predetermined adjustments of the loan interest rate at regular intervals based on an established index. The interest rate is adjusted at each interval to a rate equivalent to the index value plus a predetermined spread, or margin, over the index, usually subject to per-interval and to life-of-loan interest rate and/or payment rate caps.

Adjustable-rate preferred stock (ARPS)

Publicly traded issues that may be collateralized by mortgages and MBS

Adjusted balance method

Method of calculating finance charges that uses the account balance remaining after adjusting for all transactions posted during the given billing period as its basis. Related: Average daily balance method, previous balance method, past due balance method.

Adjusted basis

Price from which to calculate and derive capital gains or losses upon sale of an asset. Account actions such as any stock splits that have occurred since the initial purchase must be accounted for.

Adjusted debit balance (ADB)

The account balance for a margin account that is calculated by combining the balance owed to a broker with any outstanding balance in the special miscellaneous account, and any paper profits on short accounts.

Adjusted exercise price

Term used in options on Ginnie Mae (Government National Mortgage Association) contracts. The final exercise price of the option accounts for the coupon rates carried on Ginnie Mae mortgages. For example, if the standard GNMA mortgage has an 9% yield, the price of GNMA pools with 13% mortgages in them is altered so that the investor receives the same yield.

Adjusted gross income (AGI)

Gross income less allowable adjustments, is the income on which an individual is taxed by the federal government.

Adjusted present value (APV)

The net present value analysis of an asset if financed solely by equity (present value of unlevered cash flows), plus the present value of any financing decisions (levered cash flows). In other words, the various tax shields provided by the deductibility of interest and the benefits of other investment tax credits are calculated separately. This analysis is often used for highly leveraged transactions such as a leveraged buyout.

Adjustment bond

A bond issued in exchange for outstanding bonds when a corporation facing bankruptcy is recapitalized.

Administrative Exception Notes

CoCom controls exports at three levels, depending on the item and the proposed destination. At the lowest level, "national discretion" (also called "administrative exception"), a member nation may approve the export on its own, but CoCom must be notified after the fact. Administrative exception notes are appended to list categories to describe commodities that can be approved solely at national discretion.

Administrative Notes

See Administrative Exception Notes.

Administrative pricing rules

IRS rules used to allocate income on export sales to a foreign sales corporation.

Administrative Protective Order

An Administrative Protective Order, APO, is used to protect proprietary data that is obtained during an administrative proceeding. Within Commerce, APO is most frequently used in connection with Antidumping and Countervailing Duty investigations to prohibit opposing counsel from releasing data. The term is also applied in connection with civil enforcement of export control laws to protect against the disclosure of sensitive national security information and information provided by companies being investigated for violations.

Administrative Review

Each year, beginning on the anniversary of the date of publication of an antidumping duty order, the Commerce Department's International Trade Administration is required to review and determine the amount of any antidumping duty, if an interested party requests such a review. The results of this review are published in the Federal Register noting any antidumping duty to be assessed, estimated duty to be deposited, or suspended investigation to be resumed. See: Tariff Act of 1930.

ADR

See: American Depository Receipt.

ADS

See: American Depository Share.

Ad Valorem

Literally: according to value. Any charge, tax, or duty that is applied as a percentage of value.

Ad Valorem Equivalent

AVE is the rate of duty which would have been required on dutiable imports under that item, if the United States customs value of such imports were based on the United States port of entry value.

Advance

Increase in the market price of stocks, bonds, commodities, or other assets.

Advance against documents

A loan on the security of the documents covering the shipments.

Advance commitment

A promise to sell an asset before the seller has lined up purchase of the asset. This seller can offset risk by purchasing a futures contract to fix the sales price approximately.

Advance Computerized Execution System (ACES)

Refers to the Advance Computerized Execution System, run by Nasdaq. ACES automates trades between order entry and market maker firms that have established trading relationships with each other. Securities are designated as specified for automatic execution.

Advanced Technology Products

About 500 of some 22,000 commodity classification codes used in reporting U.S. merchandise trade are identified as "advanced technology" codes and they meet the following criteria:

— The code contains products whose technology is from a recognized high technology field (e.g., biotechnology);

— These products represent leading edge technology in that field; and

— Such products constitute a significant part of all items covered in the selected classification code.

Advance Freight

Partial payment of the bill of lading freight in advance; in other respects is the same as guaranteed freight.

Advance funded pension plan

A pension plan in which funds are set aside in advance of the date of retirement.

Advancement

Money or property given to a person by the deceased before death and intended as an advance against the beneficiary's share in the will.

Advance refunding

In the context of municipal bonds, refers to the sale of new bonds (the refunding issue) before the first call date of old bonds (the issue to be refunded). The refunding issue usually specifies a rate lower than the issue to be refunded, and the proceeds are invested, usually in government securities, until the higher-rate bonds become callable. See: Refunding escrow deposits.

Adverse opinion

An independent auditor's opinion expressing that a firm's financial statements do not reflect the company's position accurately. See also: Qualified opinion.

Adverse selection

Refers to a situation in which sellers have relevant information that buyers lack (or vice versa) about some aspect of product quality.

Advising bank

A bank, operating in the exporter's country, that handles letters of credit for a foreign bank by notifying the exporter that the credit has been opened in his or her favor. The advising bank fully informs the exporter of the conditions of the letter of credit without necessarily bearing responsibility for payment.

Advisory capacity

A term indicating that a shipper's agent or representative is not empowered to make definitive decisions or adjustment without approval of the group or individual represented. See for comparison purpose Without reserve.

Advisory Committee on Export Policy

The Advisory Committee on Export Policy, ACEP, is an interagency dispute resolution body that operates at the Assistant Secretary level. ACEP is chaired by Commerce; membership includes the Departments of Defense, Energy, and State, the Arms Control and Disarmament Agency, and the intelligence community. Disputes not resolved by the ACEP must be addressed by the cabinet-level Export Administration Review Board within specific timeframes set forth under National Security Directive 53.

Advisory Committee on Trade Policy and Negotiations

The ACTPN is a group (membership of 45; two-year terms) appointed by the President to provide advice on matters of trade policy and related issues, including trade agreements. The 1974 Trade Act requires the ACTPN's establishment and broad representation of key economic sectors affected by trade. Below the ACTPN are seven policy committees: SPAC (Services Policy Advisory Committee), INPAC (Investment), IGPAC (Intergovernmental), IPAC (Industry), APAC (Agriculture), LAC (Labor), and DPAC (Defense). Below the policy committees are sectoral, technical, and functional advisory committees.

Advisory letter

A newsletter offering financial advice to its readers.

Advisory Notes

See Administrative Exception Notes.

Advocacy Center

The Advocacy Center, established in November 1993, facilitates high-level U.S. official advocacy to assist U.S. firms competing for major projects and procurements worldwide. The Center is directed by the Trade Promotion Coordinating Committee; offices are located in the Commerce Department, Washington, D.C. Telephone: 202-482-3896; fax: 202-482-3508. See: Trade Promotion Coordinating Committee.

AE

The two-character ISO 3166 country code for UNITED ARAB EMIRATES.

AED

The ISO 4217 currency code for United Arab Emirates Dirham.

AEX

See: Amsterdam Exchange.

AF

The two-character ISO 3166 country code for AFGHANISTAN.

AFA

The ISO 4217 currency code for Afghan Afghani.

Affidavit of Loss

A sworn statement describing the particulars and circumstances of the loss of securities. This affidavit is required before a Bond of Indemnity can be issued and the securities replaced.

Affiliate

An affiliate is a business enterprise located in one country which is directly or indirectly owned or controlled by a person of another country to the extent of

10 percent or more of its voting securities for an incorporated business enterprise or an equivalent interest for an unincorporated business enterprise, including a branch. For outward investment, the affiliate is referred to as a "foreign affiliate"; for inward investment, it is referred to as a "U.S. affiliate."

Affiliated corporation

A corporation that is an affiliate to the parent company.

Affiliated Foreign Group

An affiliated foreign group means (a) the foreign parent, (b) any foreign person, proceeding up the foreign parent's ownership chain, which owns more than 50 percent of the person below it up to and including that person which is not owned more than 50 percent by another foreign person, and (c) any foreign person, proceeding down the ownership chain(s) of each of these members, which is owned more than 50 percent by the person above it.

Affiliated person

An individual who possesses enough influence and control in a corporation as to be able to alter the actions of the corporation.

Affirmative covenant

A bond covenant that specifies certain actions the firm must take.

Affordability index

An index that measures the financial ability of consumers to purchase a home.

AFM

See: Amman Financial Market.

Africa Enterprise Fund

The AEF, operating under the International Finance Corporation, began operations in late 1989. The Fund assists small and medium-size enterprises in sub-Saharan Africa, supports investment projects, and promotes development of private enterprises in Africa to stimulate economic growth and productive employment.

African, Caribbean, and Pacific Countries

Abbreviated ACP, these are developing countries which are designated beneficiaries under the Lome, Convention. See Lome, Convention.

African Development Bank

AFDB (French: Banque Africaine de Developement) provides financing through direct loans to African member states to cover the foreign exchange costs incurred in Bank-approved development projects in those countries. Fifty-one African countries are members and ordinarily receive loans. The Republic of South Africa is the only African country not a member. The African Development Bank comprises the AfDB as well as the African Development Fund and the Nigeria Trust Fund. The Bank was established in August 1963 (began operations in July 1966), with headquarters in Abidjan, Cote d'Ivoire.

See African Development Foundation, African Development Fund, African Export-Import Bank, Development Fund for Africa, Nigeria Trust Fund.

African Development Foundation

ADF provides economic assistance to groups and institutions involved in development projects at the local level. The foundation's assistance, designed as a complement to the U.S. foreign aid program, is awarded only to native African organizations and individuals. ADF is a U.S. public corporation which was established by Congress in 1980 (became operational in 1984); headquarters are in Washington, D.C. See African Development Fund, Development Fund for Africa.

African Development Fund

The ADF (or AfDF) (French: Fonds Africain de Developement, FAD) is an affiliate of the African Development Bank (AfDB) which provides interest-free loans to African countries for projects which promote economic and social development and improve international trade among members of the AfDB. The Fund was established in July 1972 and commenced operations in 1973. See African Development Bank.

African Export-Import Bank

AFREXIMBANK offers short-term export trade financing to African exporters aimed at enhancing intra-African trade and Africa's exports. Agreement to create the bank was based on a January 1993 agreement reached in Cairo, Egypt among African governments, central banks, regional and sub-regional financial institutions and other organizations. Bank headquarters are located in Cairo, Egypt.

African Management Services Company

AMSCO provides temporary managers and management training to support the development of African companies. AMSCO works through a network of representatives in Africa; its clients include privately owned companies, public sector companies, and subsidiaries of international companies. The company was established in 1989 by the International Finance Corporation; headquarters are in Amsterdam, Netherlands. AMSCO is funded by the United Nations Development Program, the International Finance Corporation, the African Development Fund, the African

Development Bank, development institutions in several European countries, and private sector investors.

African Regional Organization for Standardization

ARSO (French: Organisation Regionale Africaine de Normalisation, ORAN) promotes and coordinates standardization, quality control, certification, and metrology practices in Africa. The Organization has been developing African Regional Standards (ARS) in nine areas: (a) general standards, (b) agricultural and food products, (c) building and civil engineering, (d) mechanical engineering and metallurgy, (e) chemistry and chemical engineering, (f) electro-technology, (g) textiles, (h) transport and communications, and (i) environmental products and pollution control. ARSO is also seeking adoption of a regional certification marking scheme and establishment of a laboratory accreditation program. ARSO was established in 1977; its headquarters are in Nairobi, Kenya. ARSO membership is restricted to official representatives of member governments.

Africa Project Development Facility

The APDF seeks to accelerate development of productive enterprises sponsored by private African entrepreneurs as a means of generating self-sustained economic growth and productive employment in Sub-Saharan Africa. The facility provides advisory services to private African entrepreneurs in preparing viable projects, works with the entrepreneurs to secure financing, and helps them obtain technical and managerial assistance to start their projects. APDF was established in 1986 as a United Nations Development Programme project — with the International Finance Corporation as executing agency and the African Development Bank as regional sponsor. The facility maintains offices in Nairobi (Kenya), Harare (Zimbabwe), and Abidjan (Côte d'Ivoire).

AFTA (ASEAN Free Trade Agreement)

See under Association of South East Asian Nations.

After acquired clause

A contractual clause in a mortgage agreement stating that any additional mortgageable property attained by the borrower after the mortgage is signed will be regarded as additional security for the obligation addressed in the mortgage.

After-hours dealing or trading

Securities trading after regular trading hours on organized exchanges.

Aftermarket

See: Secondary market.

After Sight

When a draft bears this phrase, the time begins to run from its acceptance date.

After-tax basis

The comparison basis used to analyze the net after-tax returns on a corporate taxable bond and a municipal tax-free bond.

After-tax profit margin

The ratio of net income to net sales.

After-tax real rate of return

The after-tax rate of return minus the inflation rate.

AG

The two-character ISO 3166 country code for ANTIGUA AND BARBUDAAG.

Against the box

See: Selling short against the box.

Aged fail

An account between two broker/dealers that remains intact after 30 days after the settlement date. The receiving firm must adjust its capital as it can no longer treat this account as an assets.

Agence de Coopération Culturelle et Technique

The ACCT (English: Agency for Cultural and Technical Cooperation) was created in 1970 to promote cultural and technical cooperation among French-speaking countries. Members include: Belgium, Benin, Burkina. Burundi, Canada, Central African Republic, Chad, Comoros, Congo, Djibouti, Dominica, France, Gabon, Guinea, Haiti, Côte d'Ivoire, Lebanon, Luxembourg, Mali, Mauritius, Monaco, Niger, Rwanda, Senegal, Seychelles, Togo, Tunisia, Vanuatu, Vietnam, and Zaire. ACCT also includes seven associate members: Cameroon, Egypt, Guinea-Bissau, Laos, Mauritania, Morocco, and Saint Lucia. Agency headquarters are in Paris, France.

Agencies

See: Federal agency securities.

Agency

In context of general equities, buying or selling for the account and risk of a customer. Generally, an agent, or broker, acts as intermediary between buyer and seller, taking no financial risk personally or as a firm, and charging a commission for the service. The broker represents a customer buyer/seller to a customer seller/buyer and does not act as principal for the firm's own trading account. Antithesis of principal. See: Dealer.

Agency bank

A form of organization commonly used by foreign banks to enter the US market. An agency bank cannot accept deposits or extend loans in its own name; it acts as agent for the parent bank. It is also the financial institution that issues ADRs to the general market.

Agency basis

A means of compensating the broker of a program trade solely on the basis of commission established through bids submitted by various brokerage firms.

Agency cost view

The argument that specifies that the various agency costs create a complex environment in which total agency costs are at a minimum with some, but less than 100%, debt financing.

Agency costs

The incremental costs of having an agent make decisions for a principal.

Agency for Cultural and Technical Cooperation

See Agence de Cooperation Culterelle et Technique.

Agency incentive arrangement

A means of compensating the broker of a program trade using benchmark prices for issues to be traded in determining commissions or fees.

Agency for International Development

AID was created in 1961 to administer foreign economic assistance programs of the U.S. Government. AID has field missions and representatives in approximately 70 developing countries in Africa, Latin America, the Caribbean, and the Near East.

Agency pass-throughs

Mortgage pass-through securities whose principal and interest payments are guaranteed by government agencies, such as the Government National Mortgage Association (Ginnie Mae), Federal Home Loan Mortgage Corporation (Freddie Mac), and Federal National Mortgage Association(Fannie Mae).

Agency problem

Conflicts of interest among stockholders, bondholders, and managers.

Agency securities

Securities issued by federally related institutions and U.S. government-sponsored entities. Such agencies were created to reduce borrowing costs for certain sectors of the economy, such as agriculture.

Agency theory

The analysis of principal-agent relationships, in which one person, an agent, acts on behalf of another person, a principal.

Agent

The decision-maker in a principal-agent relationship.

Agent/Distributor Service

The Agent/Distributor Service, ADS, is an International Trade Administration (ITA) fee-based service which locates foreign import agents and distributors. ADS provides a custom search overseas for interested and qualified foreign representatives on behalf of a U.S. exporter. Officers abroad conduct the search and prepare a report identifying up to six foreign prospects that have examined the U.S. firm's product literature and have expressed interest in representing the U.S. firm's products.

Aggregate exercise price

The exercise price multiplied by the number of shares in a put or call contract. The option premium is excluded in the aggregate exercise price. In the case of options traded on debt instruments, the aggregate exercise price is the exercise price of the underlying security multiplied by its face value.

Aggregation

Process in corporate financial planning whereby the smaller investment proposals of each of the firm's operational units are aggregated and effectively treated as a whole.

Aggressive Growth Hedge Fund

In the context of hedge funds, a style of management that focuses primarily on equities that are expected to have strong earnings growth.

Aggressive growth mutual fund

A mutual fund designed for maximum capital appreciation that places its money in companies with high growth rates.

Aggressively

Used in context of general equities. For a customer it means working to buy or sell one's stock, with an emphasis on execution over price. For a trader it means acting in a way that puts the firm's capital at higher risk through paying a higher price, selling cheaper, or making a larger short sale or purchase than the trader would under normal circumstances.

Aging schedule

A table of accounts receivable broken down into age categories (such as 0-30 days, 30-60 days, and 60-90 days), which is used to determine if customer payments are keeping close to schedule.

Agio

Premium received by a broker from an exporter for assuming the exporter's countertrade obligations. The commission paid to the broker represents a disagio for the exporter.

Agreement

Agreement by one government to accept the accreditation of an ambassador from another government.

Agreement among underwriters

A contract among participating members of a syndicate that defines the members' proportionate liability, which is usually limited to and based on the participants' level of involvement. The contract outlines the payment schedule on the settlement date. Compare: Underwriting agreement.

Agreement corporation

Corporation chartered by a state to engage in international banking: so named because the corporation enters into an "agreement" with the Fed's Board of Governors that it will limit its activities to those permitted and Edge Act Corporation.

Agriculture Information System

AGRIS, coordinated under the auspices of the Food and Agricultural Organization, is an international cooperative bibliographic database on agricultural research, production, science, and technology. Participating countries contribute information for inclusion in AGRIS. See: National Agricultural Library.

Agricultural Marketing Service

Among its activities, the Agriculture Department's AMS is available to foreign buyers to assure that any product shipped overseas meets contract specifications. The service is operated on a user-fee basis. AMS works with the buyers to write a specification that can be certified. The requirements for USDA certification can be made apart of the purchase contract.

Agricultural Officers

Agricultural officers are embassy officials who are responsible for addressing agricultural trade policy issues and preparing reports on agricultural commodities such as rice, wheat, and dairy products. These officers promote U.S. exports by providing market information, one-on-one consultations, and facilitative contacts with foreign buyers and by sponsoring trade events, such as shows, trade missions, and seminars.

Agricultural OnLine Access

See National Agricultural Library.

Agricultural Trade and Marketing Information Center

See National Agricultural Library.

Agricultural Trade Offices

See Foreign Agricultural Service.

Ahead of itself

In context of general equities, refers to equities that are overbought or oversold on a fundamental basis.

Ahead of you

Used for listed equity securities. At the same price but entered ahead of your order/interest, usually referring to the specialist's book. See: Behind, matched orders, priority, stock ahead.

AI

The two-character ISO 3166 country code for ANGUILLAAI.

AIBD

Association of International Bond Dealers.

Aide-Mémoire

A short written summary of oral remarks made to a foreign government representative and left with that individual.

AIMR Performance Presentation Standards Implementation Committee

The Association for Investment Management and Research (AIMR) Performance Presentation Standards Implementation Committee is charged with the responsibility to interpret, revise, and update the AIMR Performance Presentation Standards (AIMR-PPS(TM) for portfolio performance presentations.

Airbus Industries Group

AIG is a supernational management organization responsible for design, development, manufacture, marketing, sales and support of selected commercial aircraft. Member countries are France, Germany, Spain, and the United Kingdom. Airbus Industry, G.I.E. is a consortium of four West European producers — Aérospatiale (France), Deutsche Aerospace Airbus GmbH (Germany), British Aerospace Airbus Ltd. (United Kingdom), and Construcciones Aeron uticas S.A. (Spain) — established as a groupement d'intérêt économique (G.I.E.) under French law.

Air Freight Consolidator

An air freight carrier that does not own or operate its own aircraft but ships its cargo with actual equipment operating carriers. Consolidators issue house air waybills to their customers and receive master air waybills from the actual carriers.

Air pocket stock

A stock whose price drops precipitously, often on the unexpected news of poor results.

Air waybill (AWB)

A bill of lading that covers both domestic and international flights trasnporting goods to a specified destination. This is a non-negotiable instrument of air transport that serves as a receipt for the shipper, indicating that the carrier has accepted the goods listed and obligates itself to carry the consignment to the airport of destination according to specified conditions. See also Inland bill of lading, Ocean bill of lading, and Through bill of lading.

Aktiengesellschaft (AG)

AG (German, meaning: "stock company") is a corporation with a separate legal personality which must have at least five partners. The firm name usually reflects the activities of the company and must include "AG."

AL

The two-character ISO 3166 country code for ALBANIA.

Alien corporation

A company incorporated under the laws of a foreign country regardless of where the company conducts its operations.

ALL

The ISO 4217 currency code for Albanian Lek.

All equity rate

The discount rate that reflects only the business risks of a project, distinct from the effects of financing.

Alliance for Mutual Growth (AMG)

The U.S.-ASEA N Alliance for Mutual Growth (AMG) was launched in 1993. The AMG seeks to tie commercial initiatives to U.S. policy priorities in the region, taking a broad view of trade promotion focusing on establishing the long-term relationships and presence necessary to succeed in ASEAN.

All in

Refers to an issuer's interest rate after accounting for commissions and various related expenses.

All-in-rate

Rate used in charging customers for accepting banker's acceptances, consisting of the discount interest rate plus the commission.

All Ordinaries Index

The major index of Australian stocks comprising 330 of the major companies listed on the Australian Stock Exchange.

All or none order (AON)

Used in context of general equities. A limited price order that is to be executed in its entirety or not at all (no partial transaction), and thus is testing the strength/conviction of the counterparty. Unlike an FOK order, an AON order is not to be treated as cancelled if not executed as soon as it is represented in the trading crowd, but instead remains alive until executed or cancelled.

The making of "all or none" bids or offers in stocks is prohibited, and the making of "all or none" bids or offers in bonds is subject to the restrictions of Rule 61. AON orders are not shown on the specialist's book because they cannot be traded in pieces. Antithesis of any-part-of order. See: FOK order.

All-in cost

Total costs, explicit and implicit.

All-or-none underwriting

An arrangement whereby a security issue is cancelled if the underwriter is unable to resell the entire issue.

All Risk Insurance

Marine cargo insurance which covers most perils except strikes, riots, civil commotion's, capture, war, seizure, civil war, piracy, loss of market, and inherent vice.

Allied member

A partner or stockholder of a firm that is a member of the NYSE, the partner or stockholder is not personally a member of the NYSE.

Alligator spread

The term used to describe a spread in the options market that generates such a large commission that the client is unlikely to make a profit even if the markets move as the investor anticipated.

Allocation-of-income rules

US tax provisions that define how income and deductions are to be allocated between domestic source and foreign source income.

Allocational efficiency

The effectiveness with which a market channels capital toward its most productive uses.

Allotment

The number of securities assigned to each of the participants in an underwriting syndicate.

All Risk Clause

An insurance provision which provides additional coverage to an Open Cargo Policy, usually for an additional premium. Contrary to its name, the clause does not protect against all risks. The more common perils it does cover are theft, pilferage, non-delivery, fresh water damage, contact with other cargo, breakage, and leakage. Inherent vice, loss of market, and losses caused by delay are not covered.

All Risks Coverage

All Risks Coverage, a type of marine insurance, is the broadest kind of standard coverage, but excludes damage caused by war, strikes, and riots. See also Marine Cargo Insurance.

Alongside

A phrase referring to the side of a ship. Goods to be delivered "alongside" are to be placed on the dock or lighter within reach of the transport ship's tackle so that they can be loaded aboard the ship. Goods are delivered to the port of embarkation, but without loading fees.

Alpha

Measure of risk-adjusted performance. An alpha is usually generated by regressing the security or mutual fund's excess return on the S&P 500 excess return. The beta adjusts for the risk (the slope coefficient). The alpha is the intercept. Example: Suppose the mutual fund has a return of 25%, and the short-term interest rate is 5% (excess return is 20%). During the same time the market excess return is 9%. Suppose the beta of the mutual fund is 2.0 (twice as risky as the S&P 500). The expected excess return given the risk is 2 x 9%=18%. The actual excess return is 20%. Hence, the alpha is 2% or 200 basis points. Alpha is also known as the Jensen Index. Related: Risk-adjusted return.

Alpha equation

Regression usually run over 36-60 months of data: Return-Treasury bill= alpha + beta (S&P 500 - Treasury bill) + error. The alpha is the intercept. Note that the benchmark does not necessarily have to be the S&P 500. A mutual fund specializing in international investment might be benchmarked to a broader world market index, such as the MSCI World Index.

Alphabet stock

Categories of common stock of a corporation associated with a particular subsidiary resulting from acquisitions and restructuring. The various alphabetical categories have different voting rights and pay dividends tied to the operating performance of the particular divisions. See also: Tracking stocks.

ALT

Alternative Trading System. This term is defined under section 301 of the U.S. Securities Act.

Alternative investments

Refers to investments in hedge funds. Many hedge funds pursue strategies that are uncommon relative to mutual funds. Examples of alternative investment strategies are: long-short equity, event driven, statistical arbitrage, fixed income arbitrage, convertible arbitrage, short bias, global macro, and equity market neutral.

Alternative Minimum Tax (AMT)

A federal tax aimed at ensuring that wealthy individuals, estates, trusts, and corporations pay a minimal level income tax. For individuals, the AMT is calculated by adding adjusted gross income to tax preference items.

Alternative mortgage instruments

Variations of mortgage instruments such as adjustable-rate and variable-rate mortgages, graduated-payment mortgages, reverse-annuity mortgages, and several seldom-used variations.

Alternative order

Used in context of general equities. Order giving a broker a choice between two courses of action, either to buy or sell, never both. Execution of one course automatically eliminates the other. An example is a combination buy limit/buy stop order, where the buy limit is below the current market and the buy stop is above. If the order is for one unit of trading, when one part of the order is executed on the occurrence of one alternative, the order on the other alternative is to be treated as cancelled. If the order is for an amount of more than one unit of trading, the number of units executed determines the amount of the alternative order to be treated as cancelled. See: Either-or order.

AM

The two-character ISO 3166 country code for ARMENIA.

AMD

The ISO 4217 currency code for Armenian Dram.

American Association of Individual Investors (AAII)

A not-for-profit organization to educate individual investors about stocks, bonds, mutual funds, and other financial instruments.

American Business Center

The ABC program provides U.S. companies which are exploring or establishing commercial opportunities in the Newly Independent States of the former Soviet Union with business services such as telephone and fax, temporary office space, market information, and assistance in making business contacts. An ABC operates in Bratislava, Slovakia under the direction of the Commerce Department's International Trade Administration in cooperation with the Agency for International Development. Additional centers are being opened in Russia, the Ukraine, Kazakhstan, Uzbekistan.

American Business Initiative

The ABI, or American Business and Private Sector Development Initiative for Eastern Europe, emphasizes the export of American telecommunications, energy, environment, housing, and agriculture products and services to Eastern European countries.

American Depository Receipt (ADR)

Certificates issued by a US depository bank, representing foreign shares held by the bank, usually by a branch or correspondent in the country of issue. One ADR may represent a portion of a foreign share, one share or a bundle of shares of a foreign corporation. If the ADR's are "sponsored," the corporation provides financial information and other assistance to the bank and may subsidize the administration of the ADR "Unsponsored" ADRs do not receive such assistance. ADRs are subject to the same currency, political, and economic risks as the underlying foreign share. Arbitrage keeps the prices of ADRs and underlying foreign shares, adjusted for the SDR/ordinary ratio essentially equal. American depository shares (ADS) are a similar form of certification.

American Depository Receipt Fees

Fees associated with the creating or releasing of ADRs from ordinary shares, charged by the commercial banks with correspondent banks in the international sites.

American Depository Receipt Ratio

The number of ordinary shares into which an ADR can be converted.

American Depository Share (ADS)

Foreign stock issued in the US and registered in the ADR system.

American Institute in Taiwan

The AIT is a non-profit corporation that represents U.S. commercial, cultural, and other interests in Taiwan in lieu of an embassy. In 1979, the United States terminated formal diplomatic relations with Taiwan when it recognized the People's Republic of China as the sole legal government of China. AIT was authorized to continue commercial, cultural and other relations between the United States and Taiwan. AIT headquarters are located in Arlington, Virginia; constituent offices are in Taipei and Kaohsiung, Taiwan. See Coordination Council for North American Affairs.

American option

An option that may be exercised at any time up to and including the expiration date. Related: European option

American shares

Securities certificates issued in the US by a transfer agent acting on behalf of the foreign issuer. The certificates represent claims to foreign equities.

American Stock Exchange (AMEX)

Stock exchange with the third highest volume of trading in the US Located at 86 Trinity Place in downtown Manhattan. The bulk of trading on AMEX consists of index options (computer technology index, institutional index, major market index) and shares of small to medium-sized companies are predominant. Recently merged with Nasdaq See: Curb.

American-style option

An option contract that can be exercised at any time between the date of purchase and the expiration date. Most exchange-traded options are American style.

American Traders Index

The American Traders Index, ATI, is the U.S. and Foreign Commercial Service headquarters compilation of individual US&FCS domestic client files, for use by overseas posts to generate mailing lists.

AMEX

See: American Stock Exchange.

AMG

See under Alliance for Mutual Growth.

Amman Financial Market (AFM)

Established in 1976, the AFM is the only stock exchange in Jordan.

Amman Stock Exchange

The only agency authorized as a formal market for trading securities in Jordan.

Amortization

The repayment of a loan by installments.

Amortization factor

The pool factor implied by the scheduled amortization assuming no prepayments.

Amortizing interest rate swap

Swap in which the principal or notional amount rises (falls) as interest rates rise (decline).

Amount outstanding and in circulation

All currency issued by the Bureau of the Mint and intended as a medium of exchange. Coins sold by the Bureau of the Mint at premium prices are not included; uncirculated coin sets sold at face value plus handling charge are included.

AMPS

See: Auction Market Preferred Stock.

Amsterdam Exchange (AEX)

Exchange that comprises the AEX-Effectenbeurs, the AEX-Optiebeurs (formerly the European Options Exchange or EOE) and the AEX-Agrarische Termijnmarkt. AEX-Data Services is the operating company responsible for the dissemination of data from the Amsterdam Exchange via its integrated Mercury 2000 system.

AMTEL

Used in context of general equities. In-house message system entered and displayed through Quotron A page.

AN

The two-character ISO 3166 country code for NETHERLANDS ANTILLES.

Analyst

Employee of a brokerage or fund management house who studies companies and makes buy-and-sell recommendations on stocks of these companies. Most specialize in a specific industry.

Andean Development Corporation

See Andean Group.

Andean Group

The Andean Group (Spanish: Grupo Andino; sometimes referred to as Pacto Andino or Cørporation Adino de Fomento; formal reference is Acuerdo de Cartegana in recognition of the Group's establishment in Cartegena in October 1969) is an association of Latin American countries which promotes regional economic integration and political cooperation among themselves. Members include Bolivia, Colombia, Ecuador, Peru, and Venezuela; Chile withdrew in January 1976. Headquarters are in Lima, Peru. The Corporaciøn Andina de Fomentø, CAF (English: Andean Development Corporation) supports economic integration among members of the Andean Group by encouraging specialization, distribution of investments and by providing financial and technical help. The CAF was founded in 1968, began operations in 1970; headquarters are in Caracas, Venezuela.

Andean Pact

The Andean Pact was established in 1969 when Bolivia, Colombia, Ecuador and Peru signed the Cartagena Agreement. Chile was an original member but exited in 1976 to pursue an independent economic program. Venezuela joined in 1973. The original goal of the Cartagena Agreement was to promote economic self-sufficiency within the region. Members were never able to fully implement the Cartagena Agreement and virtually abandoned multilateral discussions as Latin America's economic conditions worsened during the 1980s. Broadly, the Andean Pact of the 1990s is to encourage the growth of international competitive industries and to promote increased integration of the Andean region with the global economy.

Andean Reserve Fund

The Andean Reserve Fund (Spanish: Fondo Andina de Reservas), associated with the Andean Group, was established to strengthen the balance of payments positions of member countries by offering credit, guarantee loans, and promoting compatibility among members' monetary policies. Headquarters are in Bogota, Colombia.

Andean Trade Initiative

The ATI is the trade element in U.S. drug policy. See Andean Trade Preference Act.

Andean Trade Preference Act (ATPA)

The ATPA is a unilateral trade benefit program designed to promote economic development through private sector initiative in the four Andean countries of Bolivia, Colombia, Ecuador, and Peru. The ATPA encourages alternatives to coca cultivation and production by offering broader access to the U.S. market. The Act also seeks to stimulate investment in nontraditional sectors and to diversify the Andean countries' export base. The primary provision of the program is expanded duty-free entry into the United States. The Administration must determine each country's eligibility based on criteria set forth in the Act. Bolivia, Colombia, Ecuador, and Peru have been designated as beneficiaries. The ATPA became effective in December 1991 and is due to expire in December 2001. The Act requires periodic assessments of the impact of the trade preferences by the U.S. International Trade Commission and the U.S. Department of Labor.

And interest

An indication that the buyer will receive accrued interest in addition to the price quoted for a bond.

ANG

The ISO 4217 currency code for Netherlands Antilles Guilder.

Angel

An investment-grade bond. Antithesis to fallen angel. In the context of venture capital, the first investor.

Angels

Individuals providing venture capital.

Ankle biter

Stock issued with a market capitalization of less than $500 million.

Annex

See International Agreements.

Announcement date

Date on which particular news concerning a given company is announced to the public. Used in event studies, which researchers use to evaluate the economic impact of events of interest.

Annual basis

The technique in statistics of taking a figure covering a period of less than one year and extrapolating it to cover a full one year period. The process is known as annualizing.

Annual effective yield

See: Annual percentage yield.

Annual exclusion

A tax rule allowing the deduction of certain income from taxation.

Annual fund operating expenses

For investment companies, the management fee and "other expenses," including the expenses for maintaining shareholder records, providing shareholders with financial statements, and providing custodial and accounting services. For 12b-1 funds, selling and marketing costs are also included.

Annualized gain

If stock X appreciates 1.5% in one month, the annualized gain for that stock over a twelve month period is 121.5% = 18%. Compounded over the 12 month period, the gain is (1.015)^12 -1 = 19.6%.

Annualized holding-period return

The annual rate of return that when compounded t times generates the same t-period holding return as actually occurred from period 1 to period t.

Annualizing

See: Annual basis.

Annual meeting

Meeting of stockholder held once a year at which the managers of a company report to the stockholders on the year's results.

Annual percentage rate (APR)

The periodic rate times the number of periods in a year. For example, a 5% quarterly return has an APR of 20%.

Annual percentage yield (APY)

The effective, or true, annual rate of return. The APY is the rate actually earned or paid in one year, taking into account the effect of compounding. The APY is calculated by taking one plus the periodic rate and raising it to the number of periods in a year. For example, a 1% per month rate has an APY of 12.68% (1.01^12 -1).

Annual rate of return

There are many ways of calculating the annual rate of return. If the rate of return is calculated on a monthly basis, we sometimes multiply this by 12 to express an annual rate of return. This is often called the annual percentage rate (APR). The annual percentage yield (APY), includes the effect of compounding interest.

Annual renewable term insurance

See: Term insurance.

Annual report

Yearly record of a publicly held company's financial condition. It includes a description of the firm's operations, as well as balance sheet, income statement, and cash flow statement information. SEC rules require that it be distributed to all shareholders. A more detailed version is called a 10-K.

Annual Return

This is a document, required by the government of many countries, providing certain details about the company. It often includes details of members, directors, the address of the company and sometimes some financial information.

Annuitant

An individual who receives benefits from an annuity.

Annuitize

To commence a series of payments from the capital that has accumulated in an annuity. The payments may be a fixed amount, for a fixed period of time, or for a lifetime.

Annuity

A regular periodic payment made by an insurance company to a policyholder for a specified period of time.

Annuity certain

An annuity that pays a specific amount on a monthly basis for a set amount of time.

Annuity due

An annuity with n payments, where the first payment is made at time $t = 0$, and the last payment is made at time $t = n - 1$.

Annuity factor

Present value of $1 paid for each of t periods.

Annuity in arrears

An annuity with a first payment one full period hence, rather than immediately.

Annuity starting date

The date when an annuitant starts receiving payments from an annuity.

Anticipated holding period

The period of time an individual expects to hold an asset.

Anticipation

Paying what is owed before it is due (usually to save interest charges).

Anticipatory Countertrade

Advance purchases of goods and services from a customer's country that a supplier undertakes, or causes, in expectation of a future sale linked to countertrade requirements. Such proactive purchases may not receive countertrade credit at the time of the export sale unless prior approval by the host country authorities is secured, tying the two import/export transactions.

Antidilutive effect

Result of a transaction that increases earnings per common share (e.g., by decreasing the number of shares outstanding).

Antidumping

Antidumping, as a reference to the system of laws to remedy dumping, is defined as a converse of dumping. See Dumping.

Antidumping/Countervailing Duty System

The Antidumping/Countervailing Duty System, a part of Customs' Automated Commercial System, contains a case reference database and a statistical reporting system to capture data for International Trade Commission reports on antidumping and countervailing duties assessed and paid.

Antidumping Duty

A duty assessed on imported merchandise which is subject to an antidumping duty order. The antidumping duty is assessed on an entry-by-entry basis in an amount equal to the difference between the United States price of that entry and the foreign market value of such or similar merchandise at the time the merchandise was sold to the United States. See: Tariff act of 1930.

Antidumping Duty Order

A notice issued following final determination of sales at less than fair value and material injury, or threat of material injury, providing for the imposition of antidumping duties. See Tariff Act of 1930.

Antidumping Investigation Notice

The notice published in the Federal Register announcing the initiation of an antidumping investigation. An investigation must be initiated within 20 days of the filing of a valid petition. See Tariff Act of 1930.

Antidumping Petition

A petition filed on behalf of an affected United States industry, alleging that foreign merchandise is being sold in the United States at "less than fair value" and that such sales are causing or threatening material injury to, or materially retarding the establishment of a United States industry. Commerce regulations (19 CFR 353) and International Trade Commission regulations (19CFR 207) specify the information a petition should contain. See: Tariff Act of 1930.

Antigreenmail

Greenmail refers to the agreement between a large shareholder and a company in which the shareholder agrees to sell his stock back to the company, usually at a premium, in exchange for the promise not to seek control of the company for a specified period of time. Antigreenmail provisions prevent such arrangements unless the same repurchase offer is made to all shareholders or approved a shareholder vote. There are some states that have antigreenmail laws.

Anti-Persistence

In R/S Analysis, an anti-persistent time series reverses itself more often than a random series would. If the system had been up in the previous period, it is more likely that it will be down in the next period and vice versa. Also called pink noise, or 1/f noise. See: Persistence, R/S Analysis, Hurst Exponent, Joseph Effect, Noah Effect.

Antitrust laws

Legislation established by the federal government to prevent the formation of monopolies and to regulate trade.

Any-interest-date

A call provision in a municipal bond indenture that establishes the right of redemption for the issuer on any interest payment due date.

Any-or-all bid

Often used in risk arbitrage. Takeover bid in which the acquirer offers to pay a set price for all outstanding shares of the target company, or any part thereof; contrasts with two-tier bid.

Any-part-of order

In context of general equities, order to buy or sell a quantity of stock in pieces if necessary. Antithesis of an all-or-none order (AON).

AO

The two-character ISO 3166 country code for ANGOLA.

AON

See: All or none order.

AOR

The ISO 4217 currency code for Angolan Reajustado Kwanza.

AOS

See: Automated Order System.

APEC

See under Asia-Pacific Economic Cooperation.

Apparent Consumption

An estimate of domestic consumption calculated as product shipments plus imports minus exports.

Appraisal ratio

The signal-to-noise ratio of an analyst's forecasts. The ratio of alpha to residual standard deviation.

Appraisal rights

A right of shareholders in a merger to demand the payment of a fair price for their shares, as determined independently.

Appreciation

Increase in the value of an asset.

Appropriation request

Formal request for funds for capital investment project.

Approved list

A list of equities and other investments that a financial institution or mutual fund is approved to make. See: Legal list.

APR

See: Annual Percentage Rate.

APS

Auction Preferred Stock. A type of Dutch Auction Preferred Stock (Goldman Sachs product).

APT

See: Arbitrage Pricing Theory.

APT

See: Automated Pit Trading.

APV

See: Adjusted Present Value.

APY

See: Annual Percentage Yield.

AQ

The two-character ISO 3166 country code for ANTARCTICA.

AR

(1) See: Auto-Regressive. (2) The two-character ISO 3166 country code for ARGENTINA.

Arab-African International Bank

The AAIB is a pan-Arab consortium incorporated in 1964 as a self-governing autonomous entity between the Ministry of Finance of Kuwait and the Central Bank of Egypt; each of which as co-founders hold 49.37% of the Bank's shares. A New York branch of the AAIB was established in 1981 to facilitate the financing of trade between North America and the Middle East. AAIB headquarters are in Cairo.

Arab Bank for Economic Development in Africa

The ABEDA (French: Banque Arabe pour le Dévelopement Economique en Afrique — BADEA) was created by the League of Arab States in November 1973 (began operations in March 1975) to promote economic and technical cooperation between Arab and African states. Members include: Algeria, Bahrain, Egypt, Iraq, Jordan, Kuwait, Lebanon, Libya, Mauritania, Morocco, Oman, Qatar, Saudi Arabia, Sudan, Syria, Tunesia, the United Arab Emirates, and the Palestine Liberation Organization. Bank headquarters are in Khartoum, Sudan.

Arab Cooperation Council

The ACC was created in 1989 to promote economic cooperation and integration. Members include Egypt, Iraq, Jordan, and North Yemen. The ACC, partly intended as a counterpart to Gulf Cooperation Council, was created one day subsequent to the establishment of the Arab Maghreb Union.

Arab Fund for Economic and Social Development

AFESD promotes regional economic integration and social development in Arab states. Members include: Algeria, Bahrain, Djibouti, Egypt, Iraq, Jordan, Kuwait, Lebanon, Libya, Mauritania, Morocco, Oman, Qatar, Saudi Arabia, Somalia, Sudan, Syria, Tunisia, the United Arab Emirates, Yemen, and the Palestine Liberation Organization. The Fund, associated with the League of Arab States, started operations in February 1972; headquarters are in Safat, Kuwait.

Arab International Bank

The AIB provides financing to support development of foreign trade among member nations and other Arab states. The Bank was established in October 1971; headquarters are in Cairo, Egypt. Member include: the governments of Oman, Qatar, and United Arab Emirates, as well as the Central Bank of Egypt, and the Libyan Arab Foreign Bank.

Arab League

See League of Arab States.

Arab Maghreb Union

The AMU (French: Union du Maghreb Arabe, UMA) encompasses Algeria, Libya, Mauritania, Morocco, and Tunisia. The Union was established in February 1989 to foster integration of the Maghreb economy. The Union also seeks to join the AMU and the Gulf Cooperation Council states in a common market.

Arab Monetary Fund

The AMF, originally aimed at correcting chronic deficits in the balance of payments in most member states, promotes Arab integration in monetary and economic affairs. The Fund's priorities have included: (a) addressing payments imbalances, (b) creating capital markets, (c) stabilizing exchange rates, and (d) eliminating payments and trade restrictions. Members include: Algeria, Bahrain, Egypt, Iraq, Jordan, Kuwait, Lebanon, Libya, Mauritania, Morocco, Oman, Qatar, Saudi Arabia, Somalia, Sudan, Syria, Tunisia, the United Arab Emirates, Yemen, and the Palestine Liberation Organization. The Fund was created in 1976 (began operating in April 1977); headquarters are in Abu Dhabi, United Arab Emirates. See: Arab Trade Financing Program.

Arab Trade Financing Program

The ATFP promotes trade among Arab countries and exports from Arab countries. The Program was established in 1989 by the Arab Monetary Fund; headquarters are in Abu Dhabi, United Arab Emirates.

Arbitrage

The buying of foreign exchange, securities, or commodities in one market and the simultaneous selling in another market, in terms of a third market. By this manipulation a profit is made because of the difference in the rates of exchange or in the prices of securities or commodities involved.

Arbitrage bonds

Municipality issued bonds issued intended to gain an interest rate advantage by refunding a higher-rate bond in ahead of their call date. Lower-rate refunding issue proceeds are invested in Treasuries until the first call date of the higher-rate issue.

Arbitrage-free option-pricing models

Yield curve option-pricing models.

Arbitrage Pricing Theory (APT)

An alternative model to the capital asset pricing model developed by Stephen Ross and based purely on arbitrage arguments. The APT implies that there are multiple risk factors that need to be taken into account when calculating risk-adjusted performance or alpha.

Arbitrage Trading Program (ATP)

See: Program trading.

Arbitrageur

One who profits from the differences in price when the same, or extremely similar, security, currency, or commodity is traded on two or more markets. The Arbitrageur profits by simultaneously purchasing and selling these securities to take advantage of pricing differentials (spreads) created by market conditions. See: Risk arbitrage, convertible arbitrage, index arbitrage, and international arbitrage.

ARCH

See: Auto-Regressive Conditional Heteroskedasticity.

Are you open?

Used in context of general equities. "Can a new customer still participate on opposing side of the trade from that which the first customer initiated?", Inquiring as to whether any portion of that trade is still available See: Open.

Arithmetic average (mean) rate of return

Arithmetic mean return.

Arithmetic mean return

An average of the subperiod returns, calculated by summing the subperiod returns and dividing by the number of subperiods.

Arizona Stock Exchange

A single price auction exchange for equity trading that allows anonymous buyers and sellers to trade at low transaction costs.

ARM

See: Adjustable-rate mortgage.

Arms Control and Disarmament Agency

ACDA is an independent agency within the State Department. ACDA participates in interagency working groups that discuss export license applications requiring dispute resolution. ACDA is interested in dual-use license applications from a non-proliferation perspective — anything that could impact on the proliferation of missiles, chemical and biological weapons, and nuclear weapons. ACDA's positions need not be consonant with those of State. The Agency was created in 1961, has about 200-to-250 staff, and has a fairly substantial and growing technology transfer and export control function. The Director is the principal arms control adviser to the Secretary of State, the President and the NSC on conventional arms transfer, commercial sales of munitions; nuclear, missile, chemical and biological warfare; East-West military munitions issues, CoCom, and negotiating MOUs with the 3rd world on strategic trade.

Arm's length price

The price at which a willing buyer and a willing unrelated seller would freely agree to transact or a trade between related parties that is conducted as if they were unrelated, so that there is no conflict of interest in the transaction.

Arms index

Also known as a TRading INdex (TRIN). The index is usually calculated as the number of advancing issues divided by the number of declining issues. This, in turn, is divided by the advancing volume divided by the declining volume. If there is considerably more advancing volume relative to declining volume this will tend to reduce the index (i.e. increase the denominator). Hence, a value less than 1.0 is bullish while values greater than 1.0 indicate bearish demand. The index often is smoothed with a simple moving average.

Around us

Used in context of general equities. See: Away from you.

ARPS

(1) See: Adjustable-rate preferred stock. (2) See: Auction rate preferred stock.

ARR

See: Average rate of return.

Arrangement on Guidelines for Officially Supported Export Credits

The Arrangement is an international agreement under Organization for Economic Cooperation and Development auspices governing the conditions — such as interest rate, repayment term, and cash down payment — of medium- and long-term official export credit; it does not apply to strictly private credit. For example, the Arrangement specifies how governments relate the interest rate on their export credits to market levels. Though informal and non-enforceable, Arrangement guidelines are regularly observed by the 22 OECD member governments that are "Participants" to the agreement.

Arrearage

In the context of investments, refers to the amount by which interest on bonds or dividends on cumulative preferred stock is due and unpaid.

ARS

The ISO 4217 currency code for Argentinan Peso.

Articles of incorporation

Legal document establishing a corporation and its structure and purpose.

Articles and Memorandum of Association

See Association.

Artificial currency

A currency substitute, e.g., special drawing rights (SDRs).

Artificial Intelligence

The creation of models that mimic thought processes. See: Neural Networks, Fuzzy Logic, and Genetic Algorithms.

AS

The two-character ISO 3166 country code for AMERICAN SAMOA.

Ascending tops

A chart pattern that depicts that each peak in a security's price over a period of time is higher than the preceding peak. Antithesis of descending tops.

ASE

See: Athens Stock Exchange.

ASEAN

See under Association of South East Asian Nations.

ASEAN Free Trade Area

The Association of Southeast Asian Nations (ASEAN) agreed in January 1992 to create a free trade area (ASEAN Free Trade Area, or AFTA) with use of a common effective preferential tariff. Under the agreement ASEAN members will cut tariff rates within 15 years of its start date of January 1994. Manufactured goods from 15 sectors designated as "fast track" are subject to tariff reduction to 0-5 percent within 10 years, and seven years if the starting rates were already below 20 percent. "Fast track" sectors include vegetable oils, cement, chemicals, pharmaceuticals, fertilizer, plastics, rubber products, leather products, pulp, textiles, ceramic and glass products, gems and jewelry, copper cathodes, electronics, and wooden and tartan furniture. See: Association of Southeast Asian Nations.

Asian Clearing Union

The ACU promotes regional trade and economic cooperation, including arrangements to conserve foreign exchange and encourage domestic currencies in trade. Members include Bangladesh, India, Iran, Myanmar, Nepal, Pakistan, and Sri Lanka; Bhutan, Malaysia, the Peoples' Republic of China, the Philippines, Thailand, and Vietnam have expressed interest in membership. The Union was established in 1974; headquarters are in Tehran, Iran.

Asian Currency Units (ACU)

Dollar deposits held in Singapore or other Asian centers.

Asian Development Bank

The ADB helps finance economic development in developing countries in the Asian and Pacific area through the provision of loans on near-market terms, with its Ordinary Capital Resources (OCR), and on concessional terms, through the Asian Development Fund (ADF). The ADB was established in 1965 (began operating in December 1966); headquarters are in Manila, Philippines. See Asian Development Fund.

Asian Development Fund

The ADF (or AsDF), an affiliate of the Asian Development Bank, lends funds on concessionary terms to the Bank's least developed member countries. See Asian Development Bank.

Asian Dollars

U.S. dollars deposited in Asia and the Pacific Basin. See Eurodollars.

Asian dollar market

Asian banks that collect deposits and make loans denominated in US dollars.

Asian option

Option based on the average price of the underlying assets during the life of the option.

Asia Pacific Economic Cooperation (APEC)

APEC, established in November 1989, is an informal grouping of Asia Pacific countries that provides a forum for Ministerial level discussion of a broad range of economic issues. APEC includes the six ASEAN countries (Brunei, Indonesia, Malaysia, Philippines, Singapore, and Thailand), plus: Australia, Canada, China, Hong Kong, Japan, New Zealand, South Korea, Taiwan, and the United States.

Ask

This is the quoted ask, or the lowest price an investor will accept to sell a stock. Practically speaking, this is the quoted offer at which an investor can buy shares of stock; also called the offer price.

Asked price

In context of general equities, price at which a security or commodity is offered for sale on an exchange or in the OTC Market.

Asked to bid/offer

Used in context of general equities. Usually a seller (buyer) looking to aggressively sell (buy) stock, usually asking for a capital commitment from an investment bank.

Asociaciòn Latinoamericana de Institutiones Financieras de Desarrollo

See Latin American Association of Development Financing Institutions.

Asociación Latinoamericana de Integración

See Latin American Integration Association.

Aspirin

Australian Stock Price Riskless Indexed Notes. Zero-coupon four-year bonds repayable at face value plus the percentage increase by which the Australian stock index of all ordinaries (common stocks) rises above a predefined level during the given period.

Assay

Metal purity test to confirm that the metal meets the standards for trading on a commodities exchange (commodities exchange center).

Assessed valuation

The value assigned to property by a municipality for the purpose of tax assessment. Such an assessed valuation is important to investors in municipal bonds that are backed by property taxes.

Assessment

The imposition of antidumping duties on imported merchandise. See: Tariff Act of 1930.

Asset

Any possession that has value in an exchange.

Asset activity ratios

Ratios that measure how effectively the firm is managing its assets.

Asset allocation decision

The decision regarding how an institution's funds should be distributed among the major classes of assets in which it may invest.

Asset allocation mutual fund

A mutual fund that rotates among stocks, bonds, and money market securities to maximize return on investment and minimize risk.

Asset-backed security

A security that is collateralized by loans, leases, receivables, or installment contracts on personal property, not real estate.

Asset-based financing

Methods of financing in which lenders and equity investors look principally to the cash flow from a particular asset or set of assets for a return on, and the return of, their financing.

Asset classes

Categories of assets, such as stocks, bonds, real estate, and foreign securities.

Asset-coverage test

A bond indenture restriction that permits additional borrowing if the ratio of assets to debt does not fall below a specified minimum.

Asset Depreciation Range System

A range of depreciable lives the IRS allows for particular classes of assets.

Asset/equity ratio

The ratio of total assets to stockholder equity.

Asset for asset swap

Creditors exchange the debt of one defaulting borrower for the debt of another defaulting borrower.

Asset/liability management

The task of managing the funds of a financial institution to accomplish the two goals of a financial institution: (1) to earn an adequate return on funds invested and (2) to maintain a comfortable surplus of assets beyond liabilities. Also called surplus management.

Asset management account

Account at a brokerage house, bank, or savings institution that integrates banking services and brokerage features.

Asset play

A company with assets that are not believed to be accurately reflected in its stock price, making it an attractive buy or play.

Asset pricing model

A model for determining the required or expected rate of return on an asset. Related: Capital asset pricing model and arbitrage pricing theory.

Asset stripper

A corporate raider (company A) that takes over a target company (company B) in order to sell large assets of company B to repay debt. Company A calculates that the net selling of the assets and paying off the debt, will leave the raider with assets that are worth more than what it paid for company B.

Asset substitution

Occurs when a firm invests in assets that are riskier than those that the debtholders expected.

Asset substitution problem

Arises when the stockholders substitute riskier assets for the firm's existing assets and expropriate value from the debtholders.

Asset swap

An interest rate swap used to alter the cash flow characteristics of an institution's assets in order to provide a better match with its liabilities.

Asset turnover

The ratio of net sales to total assets.

Asset value

The net market value of a corporation's assets on a per-share basis, not the market value of the shares. A company is undervalued in the market when asset value exceeds market value.

Assets

A firm's productive resources.

Assets-in-place

Property in which a firm has already invested.

Assets requirements

A common element of a financial plan that describes projected capital spending and the proposed uses of net working capital.

Assignment

The receipt of an exercise notice by an options writer that requires the writer to sell (in the case of a call) or purchase (in the case of a put) the underlying security at the specified strike price.

Assignment of proceeds

Arrangement that allows the original beneficiary of a letter of credit to pledge or turn over proceeds to another, typically end supplier.

Assimilation

The public absorption of a new issue of stocks once the stock has been completely sold by underwriter. See: Absorbed.

Associate

One associated with another in an undertaking; closely or usually connected with another party or organization with common interests, as if a partner.

Association

Articles and Memorandum of Association. In common law jurisdictions these two documents comprise the constitution of a company and govern the powers of the company to trade, issue shares, and borrow money as well as defining the relationships between the shareholders, directors and the officers of the company.

Association of African Development Finance Institutions

AADFI (French: Association des Institutions Africaines de Financement du Developement, AIAFD) promotes cooperative financing for social development in Africa and economic integration. The Association was established in March 1975; headquarters are in Abidjan, Côte d'Ivoire.

Association of African Trade Promotion Organizations

AATPO promotes inter-African trade, harmonization of commercial policies, communication among African states in trade matters, and research and training. The organization, which has about 26 members, was established in 1975 under the auspieces of the Organization for African Unity and the African Development Bank; headquarters are in Tangier, Morocco.

Association des Banques Centrales Africaines

See Association of Central African Banks.

Association of Central African Banks

ACAB (French: Association des Banques Centrales Africanines, ABCA) promotes cooperation among monetary, banking, and financial institutions in Africa. Members include two African regional banks and about 32 national banks. The Association was created in 1968; headquarters are in Dakar, Senegal.

Association of Coffee Producing Countries

See International Coffee Agreement.

Association of International Bond Dealers

The AIBD provides a forum for over 500 members from 30 countries to review international securities market matters. The primary objectives of the Association are to provide a basis for examination and discussion of questions relating to the secondary market in Eurosecurities, to issues rules governing their functions, and to maintain a close liaison between the primary and secondary markets in Eurosecurities. IABD was established in 1969; headquarters are in Zurich, Switzerland.

Association of South East Asian Nations (ASEAN)

ASEAN's rapid growth is a result of its economic integration into the ASEAN Free Trade Agreement (AFTA) and world markets, strong privatization initiatives, double digit economic growth rates, expanding purchasing power, falling market access barriers and massive infrastructure projects. By the year 2010 the ASEAN region will boast 686 million consumers, a combined GDP of U.S. $1.1 trillion and the benefit of over $1 trillion in new infrastructure projects.

Assumed interest rate

Rate of interest used by an insurance company to calculate the payout on an annuity contract.

Assumption

Becoming responsible for the liabilities of another party.

ASWP

Any Safe World Port.

ASX

See: Australian Stock Exchange.

ASX Derivatives and Options Market (ASXD)

Options market trading options on more than 50 of Australia's and New Zealand's leading companies.

Asymmetric information

Information that is known to some people but not to other people.

Asymmetric taxes

When participants in a transaction have different net tax rates.

Asymmetric volatility

Phenomenon that volatility is higher in down markets than in up markets.

Asymmetry

A lack of equivalence between two things, such as the unequal tax treatment of interest expense and dividend payments.

AT

The two-character ISO 3166 country code for AUSTRIA.

"At"/"for"

Used in context of general equities. Paramount terms used to differentiate an offering. Stock is offered at; stock is bid for. In an offering, the trading syntax followed is "Quantity-at-Price"; in a bid, the syntax followed is "Price-for-Quantity."

Athens Stock Exchange

Greece's only major securities market. Greek language only.

ATPA

See under Andean Trade Preference Act.

At par

A price equal to nominal or face value of a security. See: Par.

At risk

The exposure to the danger of economic loss. Frequently used in the context of claiming tax deductions. For example, a person can claim a tax deduction in a limited partnership if the taxpayer can show it is at risk of never realizing a profit and of losing its initial investment. See: Value at risk.

ATS

The ISO 4217 currency code for Austrian Schilling.

At the bell

In context of general equities, at the opening or close of the market. See: MOC Order.

At the close order

In the context of securities, an all or none market order that is to be executed at the closing price of the security on the exchange. If the execution cannot be made under this condition, the order is to be treated as cancelled.

In the context of futures and options, refers to a contract that is to be executed on some exchanges during the closing period, a period in which there is a range of prices.

At the figure

In context of general equities, at the whole integer price (excluding the fraction) closest to the side of the market (bid/ask) being discussed. At the full.

At the full

Used in context of general equities. At the figure.

At-the-money

An option is at the money if the strike price of the option is equal to the market price of the underlying security. For example, if xyz stock is trading at 54, then the xyz 54 option is at the money.

At the opening order

In context of general equities, market order or limited price order that is to be executed at the opening (and corresponding price) of the stock or not at all, and any such order or portion thereof not so executed is to be treated as cancelled.

Attractor

In non-linear dynamic series, an attractor defines the equilibrium level of the system. See: Point Attractor, Limit Cycle, and Strange Attractor.

Attribute bias

The tendency of stocks preferred by the dividend discount model to share certain equity attributes such as low price-earnings ratios, high dividend yield, high book value ratio, or membership in a particular industry sector.

Athens Stock Exchange (ASE)

Greece's principal stock exchange.

AU

The two-character ISO 3166 country code for AUSTRALIA.

Auction Market Preferred Stock (AMPS)

A type of Dutch Auction Preferred Stock (A Merrill Lynch product).

Auction markets

Markets in which the prevailing price is determined through the free interaction of prospective buyers and sellers, as on the floor of the stock exchange.

Auction rate preferred stock (ARPS)

Floating-rate preferred stock, whose dividend is adjusted every seven weeks through a Dutch auction.

AUD

The ISO 4217 currency code for Australian Dollar currency.

Audit

An examination of a company's accounting records and books conducted by an outside professional in order to determine whether the company is maintaining records according to generally accepted accounting principles. See: accountant's opinion.

Audit trail

Resolves the validity of an accounting entry by a step-by-step record by which accounting data can be traced to their source.

Auditor's certificate

See: Accountant's opinion.

Auditor's report

The independent accounting firm's opinion on whether the company's financial statements conform to generally accepted accounting principles.

Aunt Millie

An unsophisticated investor.

Ausfuhrkredit-Gesellschaft (AKA)

AKA (English: Export Credit Establishment) is an association of German banks which provide medium and long-term funding for exports.

(Die) Ausstellungs- und Messe-Ausschuss der Deutschen Wirtschaft (AUMA)

AUMA (German: the German Industry Council for Exhibitions and Trade Fairs) promotes exports by bringing together government, semiprivate, and private organizations in the coordination of domestic and overseas trade events. AUMA is a private organization and receives no government funds to support its general operations. The government may provide funds for special projects, such as research. AUMA also collects and distributes information to German firms on trade fairs worldwide.

Australia Group

The Australia Group, AG, is an informal forum through which 22 industrialized nations cooperate to curb proliferation of chemical and biological weapons through a supply approach. The AG's first meeting, held at the Australian Embassy in Paris in June 1986, was attended by Australia, Canada, Japan, New Zealand, the United States, and those nations that were then members of the European Community. Membership has expanded to include Norway, Portugal, Spain, Switzerland, Austria, Argentina, Finland, Hungary, Iceland, and representatives of the European Commission, the European Community's executive arm.

Australian Stock Exchange (ASX)

Australia's major securities market, formed when the six state stock exchanges (Adelaide, Brisbane, Hobart, Melbourne, Perth, and Sydney stock exchanges) were merged in 1987.

Autarky

Absence of a cross-border trade in models of international trade.

Autex

Video communication network through which brokerage houses alert institutional investors of their desire to transact block business (a purchase or sale) in a given security. Indications transmit small, medium, and large sizes only, with occasional limits mentioned. Supers are messages with specific size and price included. Both "indications" and "supers" can be only seen by customers (institutional subscribers to Autex). Trade recaps, advertised block trades entered by the dealer/subscribers, are also displayed, but can be seen by both institutions and dealers. See: Expunge, size.

Authentication

In the context of bonds, refers to the validation of a bond certificate.

Authority bond

A bond issued by a government agency or a corporation created to manage a revenue-producing public enterprise. The difference between an authority bond and a municipal bond is that margin protections may be incorporated in the authority bond contract as well as in the legislation that enables the authority.

Authority to Pay

A document comparable to a revocable letter of credit but under whose terms the authority to pay the seller stems from the buyer rather than from a bank.

Authorized shares

Number of shares authorized for issuance by a firm's corporate charter.

Autocorrelation

The correlation of a variable with itself over successive time intervals. Sometimes called serial correlation.

Automated bond system (ABS)

The computerized system that records bids and offers for inactively traded bonds until they are cancelled or executed on the NYSE.

Automated Broker Interface (ABI)

ABI, a part of Customs' Automated Commercial System, permits transmission of data pertaining to merchandise being imported into the United States. Qualified participants include brokers, importers, carriers, port authorities, and independent data processing companies referred to as service centers.

Automated Clearing House (ACH)

The Automated Clearinghouse (ACH) is a feature of the Automated Broker Interface which is a part of Customs' Automated Commercial System. The ACH combines elements of bank lock box arrangements with electronic funds transfer services to replace cash or check for payment of estimated duties, taxes, and fees on imported merchandise.

Automated Commercial System (ACS)

The Customs Service's Automated Commercial System, ACS, is a joint public-private sector computerized data processing and telecommunications system linking customhouses, members of the import trade community, and other government agencies with the Customs computer. Trade users file import data electronically, receive needed information on cargo status, and query Customs files to prepare submissions. Duties, taxes, and fees may be paid by electronic statement, through a Treasury-approved clearinghouse bank. ACS contains the import data used by Census to prepare U.S. foreign trade statistics. ACS began operating in February 1984 and includes: (a) the Automated Broker Interface, (b) the Census Interface System, (c) the Automated Manifest Systems, (d) the Bond System, (e) the In-Bond System, (f) the Cargo Selectivity System, (g) the Line Release System, (h) the Collections System, (i) the Security System, (j) the Quota System, (k) the Entry Summary Selectivity System, (l) the Entry Summary System, (m) the Automated Information Exchange, (n) the Antidumping/Countervailing Duty System, (o) the Firms System, (p) the Liquidation System, (q) the Drawback System, (r) the Fines, Penalties, and Forfeitures System, and (s) the Protest System.

Automated Customer Account Transfer (ACAT)

For transfers of securities from a non-equity trading account to your equity trading account with your broker.

Automated Export Reporting Program (AERP)

The AERP provides for electronic submission of most information required on the Shipper's Export Declaration. The program was initiated in 1969 with the intent of enabling large volume exporters to submit electronically and facilitate Census Bureau data entry and analysis. AERP was expanded in 1982 to allow freight forwarders, and again in 1985 to allow ocean carriers, to file electronically. At the beginning of fiscal year 1994, about 220 firms — accounting for 350,000 to 400,000 records a month — were participating in AERP. The program is administered by the Automated Data Reporting Branch, Foreign Trade Division, Bureau of the Census. Telephone: 301-763-7774. See Shipper's Export Declaration.

Automated Export System

Electronic filing of Shippers Export Declaration (SEDs)with US Customs prior to departure.

Automated Information Exchange (AIES)

AIES, a part of Customs' Automated Commercial System, allows for exchange of classification and value information between field units and headquarters.

Automated Manifest Systems (AMS)

AMS, a part of Customs' Automated Commercial System (ACS) controls imported merchandise from the time a carrier's cargo manifest is electronically transmitted to Customs until control is relinquished to another segment of the ACS.

Automated Order System (AOS)

Investment banks, computerized order entry system that sends single order entries to DOT (Odd-Lot) or to investment banks, floor brokers on the exchange. See: Round lot, GTC orders.

Automated Pit Trading (APT)

Introduced in 1989, APT is the LIFFE screen-based trading system that replicates the open outcry method of trading on screen. APT is used to extend the trading day for the major futures contracts as well as to provide a daytime trading environment for non-floor trading products.

Automated teller maching (ATM)

Computer-controlled terminal located on the premises of financial institutions or elsewhere, though which customers may make deposits, withdrawals or other transactions as they would through a bank teller. Other terms sometimes used to describe such terminals are customer-bank communications terminal (CBCT) and remote service unit (RSU)Groups of banks sometimes share ATM.

Automated Trade Locator Assistance Network (ATLAS)

ATLAS is a Small Business Administration-sponsored, contractor-operated, automated system which provides market research information and statistics on world markets by SIC code (and possibly harmonized system). Indirect access is available for businesses, with arrangements through the local SBA district office. ATLAS, which became operational in Spring 1993, replaced SBA's export information system (XIS).

Automatic Data Processing (ADP)

Acts as an intermediary to perform proxy services for several banks and brokers. Distributes proxy material to beneficial owners, tabulates the returned proxies, and provides the Corporation or its tabulator compiled reports of the tabulation results. ADP also distributes quarterly reports and other corporate information to the beneficial owners.

Automatic exercise

A protection procedure whereby the Options Clearing Corporation attempts to protect the holder of an expiring in-the-money option by automatically exercising the option on behalf of the holder.

Automatic extension

An automatic extension of time granted to a taxpayer to file a tax return.

Automatic funds transfer

A transfer of funds from one account or investment vehicle to another using electronic or telecommunications technology.

Automatic investment program

A program in which an investor can invest or withdraw funds automatically. A mutual fund, for example, automatically withdraw a pre determined specified amount from the investor's bank account on a regular basis.

Automatic reinvestment

See: Constant dollar plan.

Automatic stay

The restricting of liabilityholders from collection efforts related to collateral seizure. Automatically imposed when a firm files for bankruptcy under Chapter 11.

Automatic transfer service (ATS) account

A depositor's saving account from which funds may be transferred automatically to the same depositor's checking account to cover a check written or to maintain a minimum balance.

Automatic withdrawal

A mutual fund that gives shareholders the right to receive a fixed payment from dividends on a quarterly or monthly basis.

Auto Pact

An agreement on automotive products between the government of the United States and Canada that went into effect in September 1966. The pact has resulted in a large increase in bilateral automotive trade.

Autoquote

Autoquote indicative prices are generated for many of the financial options contracts traded at LIFFE using standard mathematical models as derived by Black and Scholes and Cox, Ross, Rubinstein. Autoquote calculates prices for all series by processing variables captured in real-time from other systems and trading members each time the underlying price changes. Autoquotes indicate where a series may trade, given the current level of the underlying instrument.

Autoregressive

Using past data or variable of interest to predict future values of the same variable.

Auto-Regressive (AR) Process

A stationary stochastic process where the current value of the time series is related to the past p values, where p is any integer, is called an AR(p) process. When the current value is related to the previous two values, it is an AR(2) process. An AR(1) process has an infinite memory.

Auto-Regressive Conditional Heteroskedasticity (ARCH)

A nonlinear stochastic process, where the variance is time-varying, and a function of the past variance.

ARCH processes have frequency distributions which have high peaks at the mean and fat-tails, much like fractal distributions. The Generalized ARCH (GARCH) model is also widely used. See: Fractal Distributions.

Autorité du Bassin du Niger

See Niger Basin Authority.

Availability float

Checks deposited by a company that have not yet been cleared.

Available on the way in

In context of general equities, stock is available to new customer as trade initiated by another customer is about to be consummated (on the exchange floor). Usually said to an inquiring salesperson. See: Open.

Aval

Term meaning inseparable from the financial instrument. This gives a guarantee and is abstracted from the performance of the underlying trade contract: Article 31 of the 1930 Geneva Convention of the Bills Of Exchange states that the aval can be written on the bill itself or on an allonge. US Banks are prohibited from avalizing drafts.

Avalizor

An institution or person who gives the aval.

Average

An arithmetic mean return of selected stocks intended to represent the behavior of the market or some component of it. One good example is the widely quoted Dow Jones Industrial Average, which adds the current prices of the 30 DJIA stocks, and divides the results by a predetermined number, the divisor.

Average accounting return

The average project earnings after taxes and depreciation divided by the average book value of the investment during its life.

Average (across-day) measures

An estimation of price that uses the average or representative price of a large number of trades.

Average age of accounts receivable

The weighted-average age of all the firm's outstanding invoices.

Average collection period, or days' receivables

The ratio of accounts receivables to sales, or the total amount of credit extended per dollar of daily sales (average AR/sales 365).

Average cost

In the context of investing, refers to the average cost of shares or stock bought at different prices over time.

Average cost of capital

A firm's required payout to bondholders and stockholders expressed as a percentage of capital contributed to the firm. Average cost of capital is computed by dividing the total required cost of capital by the total amount of contributed capital.

Average daily balance

A method for calculating interest in which the balance owed each day by a customer is divided by the number of days. See also: Adjusted balance method and previous balance method.

Average discount rate

Purchasers tender their competitive bids on a discount rate basis. The weighted, or adjusted, mean of all bids accepted in Treasury bill auctions.

Average down

A strategy used by investors to reduce the average cost of shares, in which the investor purchases more shares with a fixed amount of capital as the price of the shares decrease. The investor receives more shares per dollar and decreases the average price per share.

Average equity

A customer's average daily balance in a trading account at a brokerage firm.

Average life

Also referred to as the weighted-average life (WAL). The average number of years that each dollar of unpaid principal due on the mortgage remains outstanding. Average life is computed as the weighted-average time to the receipt of all future cash flows, using as the weights the dollar amounts of the principal paydowns.

Average maturity

The average time to maturity of securities held by a mutual fund. Changes in interest rates have greater impact on funds with longer average maturity.

Average rate of return (ARR)

The ratio of the average cash inflow to the amount invested.

Average tax rate

Taxes as a fraction of income; total taxes divided by total taxable income.

Average up

A strategy used by investors to lower the overall cost of shares by buying as many shares with a given amount of capital in an increasing market. Buying $1000 worth of shares at $30, $35, $40, and $45, for instance, will make the average cost of the shares $37.50.

Averaging

See: Constant dollar plan.

AW

The two-character ISO 3166 country code for ARUBA.

Away

A trade, quote, or market that does not originate with the dealer in question, e.g., "the bid is 98-10 away from me."

Away from the market

In context of general equities, out of line with the inside market at this time, such as when a bid on a limit order is lower or the offer price is higher than the current market price for the security; held by the specialist for later execution unless FOK. Antithesis of in-line.

Away from us

Used in context of general equities, to characterize role of a competing broker/dealer. Trading away from us signifies that stock is bought and/or sold with institutions using other trading firms.

Away from you

Used for listed equity securities. See: Outside of you.

AWG

The ISO 4217 currency code for Aruban Guilder.

Axe to grind

Used in context of general equities. Involvement in a security, whether through a position, order, or inquiry.

AZ

The two-character ISO 3166 country code for AZERBAIJAN.

AZM

The ISO 4217 currency code for Azerbaijani Manat.

B

Fifth letter of a Nasdaq stock descriptor specifying that issue is the Class B shares of the company.

B2B

An Internet strategy of dealing directly with businesses, rather than consumers, i.e. business to (2) business.

BA

The two-character ISO 3166 country code forBOSNIA AND HERZEGOVINA.

Baby bond

A bond with a par value of less than $1000.

Back away

In the context of general equities, to withdraw from a previously declared interest, indication, or transaction; broker-dealer's failure, as a market maker in a given security, to make good on a bid/offer for the minimum quantity.

Back fee

The fee paid on the extension date if the buyer wishes to continue the option.

Back months

In the context of futures and options trading, refers to the months of contracts with expiration dates farthest away. See farthest month.

Back office

Brokerage house clerical operations that support, but do not include, the trading of stocks and other securities. All written confirmation and settlement of trades, record keeping, and regulatory compliance happen in the back office.

Back on the shelf

In the context of general equities, permanently canceledorder/interest in a stock by a customer. See: Take a powder.

Back Order

That portion of an order which the vendor cannot deliver on schedule and which has been re-entered for shipment when available.

Back taxes

Due taxes that have not been paid on time.

Back up

(1) When bond yields rise and prices fall, the market is said to backup. (2) An investor who swaps out of one security into another of shorter current maturity is said to back up.

"Back up the truck"

In the context of general equities, "Prepare for a very large buyer."

Backdating

In the context of mutual funds, a feature allowing fundholders to use an earlier date on a letter of intent to invest in a mutual fund in exchange for a reduced sales charge, e.g. Giving retroactive value to purchases from the earlier date.

Backed in

In the context of general equities, to describe result of unanticipated events that allow for a purchase at a discount or a sale at a premium.

Back-end load fund

A mutual fund that charges investors a fee to sell (redeem) shares, often ranging from 4% to 6%. Some back-end load funds impose a full commission if the shares are redeemed within a designated length of time, such as one year. The commission decreases, the longer the investor holds the shares. The formal name for the back-end load is the contingent deferred sales charge, or CDSC

Back-testing

Creating a hypothetical portfolio performance history by applying current asset selection criteria to prior time periods.

Back-to-back financing

An intercompany loan channeled through a bank.

Back-to-back loan

A loan in which two companies in separate countries borrow each other's currency for a specific time period and repay the other's currency at an agreed-upon maturity.

Backup line

A commercial paper issuer's bank line of credit covering maturing notes if, for some reason, selling new notes to cover the maturing notes is not possible.

Backup Line of Credit

A bank assurance of funds obtained by an issuer of commercial paper to protect the CP investor from default. The issuer pays a commitment fee to the bank.

Backwardation

A market condition in which futures prices are lower in the distant delivery months than in the nearest delivery month. This may occur when the costs of storing the product until eventual delivery are effectively subtracted from the price today. The opposite of contango.

Bad debt

A debt that is written off and deemed uncollectible.

Bad delivery

Antithesis of good delivery.

Bad title

Title to property that does not distinctly confer ownership, usually in the context of real estate.

Bai-kai

Two-sided market picture, in Japanese terminology applies mainly to international equities.

Bailing out

In the context of securities, refers to selling a security or commodity quickly, regardless of the price. May occur when an investor no longer wants to sustain further losses on a stock.

Also refers to relieving an individual, corporation, or government entity in financial trouble.

Bailout bond

A bond issued by the Resolution Funding Corporation (Refcorp) to save the failing savings and loan associations in the late 1980s and early 1990s.

Baker Plan

A plan by former U.S. Treasury Secretary James Baker under which 15 principal middle-income debtor countries (the Baker 15) would undertake growth-oriented structural reforms, to be supported by increased financing from the World Bank and continued lending from commercial banks.

Balanced budget

A budget in which the income equals expenditure. See: budget.

Balanced fund

An investment company that invests in stocks and bonds. The same as a balanced mutual fund.

Balanced mutual fund

This is a fund that buys common stock, preferred stock, and bonds. The same as a balanced fund.

Balance of Payment

The balance of payments is a statistical summary of international transactions. These transactions are defined as the transfer of ownership of something that has an economic value measurable in monetary terms from residents of one country to residents of another. The transfer may involve:

(a) goods, which consist of tangible and visible commodities or products;

(b) services, which consist of intangible economic outputs, which usually must be produced, transferred, and consumed at the same time and in the same place;

(c) income on investments; and

(d) financial claims on, and liabilities to, the rest of the world, including changes in a country's reserve assets held by the central monetary authorities.

Generally, a transaction is the exchange of one asset for another — or one asset for several assets — but it may also involve a gift, which is the provision by one party of something of economic value to another party without something of economic value being received in return.

International transactions are recorded in the balance of payments on the basis of the double-entry principle used in business accounting, in which each transaction gives rise to two offsetting entries of equal value so that, in principle, the resulting credit and debit entries always balance. Transactions are generally valued at market prices and are, to the extent possible, recorded when a change of ownership occurs. Transactions in goods, services, income, and unilateral transfers constitute the current account, and transactions in financial assets and liabilities constitute the capital account.

The International Monetary Fund, which strives for international comparability, defines the balance of payments as "a statistical statement for a given period showing :

(1) transactions in goods, services, and income between an economy and the rest of the world;

(2) changes of ownership and other changes in that economy's monetary gold, special drawing rights (SDRs), and claims on and liabilities to the rest of the world; and

(3) unrequited transfers and counterpart entries that are needed to balance, in the accounting sense, any entries for the foregoing transactions and changes which are not mutually offsetting."

The U.S. balance of payments presentation does not contain a specific number that indicates an overall "balance," although several partial balances are published. In an accounting sense, an overall balance is not possible, because, the net sum of credit and debit entries in the balance of payments accounts is conceptually zero, in accordance with the principles of double-entry accounting. If the entries do not balance exactly, the net amount of missing credits or debits is entered as a statistical discrepancy in order to bring the two parts of the statement into equilibrium.

The seven balances that are currently published quarterly are:

— the balance on merchandise trade, which measures the net transfer of merchandise exports and imports;

— the balance on services, which measures the net transfer of services, such as travel, other transportation, and business, professional, and other technical services (this balance was redefined in 1990 to exclude investment income);

— the balance on goods and services, which measures the sum of the balance on merchandise trade and the balance on services;

— the balance on investment income, which measures the net transfer income on direct and portfolio investments;

— the balance on goods, services, and income, which measures the net transfer of merchandise plus services and income on direct and portfolio investment (this balance is equivalent to the pre-1990 balance on goods and services; it is also conceptually comparable to net exports of goods and services included in GNP);

— the balance on unilateral transfers (net), which measures the net value of gifts, contributions, government grants to foreign countries, and other unrequited transfers;

— the balance on current account (widely used for analysis and forecasting) which measures transactions in goods, services, income, and unilateral transfers between residents and nonresidents.

Balance of trade

Net flow of goods (exports minus imports) between two countries.

Balance on goods and services

Netting of transaction balances, including the net amount of payments of interest and dividends to foreign investors and investments, as well as receipts and payments resulting from international tourism.

Balance sheet

Also called the statement of financial condition, it is a summary of a company's assets, liabilities, and owners' equity.

Balance sheet exposure

See: Accounting exposure.

Balance sheet identity

Total assets = Total liabilities + Total stockholders' equity.

Balloon interest

In the context of serial bond issues, the elevated coupon rate on bonds with late maturity's.

Balloon maturity

Any large principal payment due at maturity for a bond or loan with or without a sinking fund requirement.

Balloon Payment

The final (large) payment that repays all the remaining principal and interest of a partially amortized or unamortized loan.

Ballot

The document distributed at the annual meeting to shareholders of record who wish to vote their shares in person.

BAM

The ISO 4217 currency code for Bosnia & Herzegovinan Convertible Mark.

BAN

See: Bond anticipation note.

Banco Centroamericano de Integracion Economico

See Central American Bank for Economic Integration.

Banco Interamericano de Desarollo

See Inter-American Development Bank.

Banco Latinoamericano de Exportaciones (BLADEX)

BLADEX (English: Latin American Export Bank) is a multinational bank which provides short- (95%+) and medium-term financing. Operations are conducted in U.S. dollars. Borrowers are primarily Latin American commercial banks of member countries which finance specific trade transactions for their customers. The bank was incorporated in 1978 (began operations in January 1979); headquarters are in Panama City, Panama. Shareholders includes Latin American central and commercial banks, international commercial banks, and the International Finance Corporation.

Banco Nacional de Comercio Exterior (BANCOMEXT)

BANCOMEXT, Mexico's national foreign trade bank, provides credits, guarantees, and promotion services to support Mexico's foreign trade. BANCOMEXT also assists Mexican importers by providing short-term loans to support importation of selected commodities and medium-term credits (up to five years) for importation of capital goods. Headquarters are in Mexico City.

Bank Advisory Committee

The Bank Advisory Committee, which in some respects has replaced the London Club, is not a structured or formal organization. The Bank Advisory Committee consists mostly of lead bankers in an individual debtor country. The lead bankers, representing the interests of the debtor country's banking industry, develop restructuring plans which the committee proposes to their government. The debtor country government, in turn, proposes the plan to foreign lending governments. See London Club.

Bank Affiliate Export Trading Company

An Export Trading Company partially or wholly owned by a banking institution as provided under the U.S. Export Trading Company Act.

Bank anticipation notes (BAN)

Notes issued by states and municipalities to obtain interim financing for projects that will eventually be funded long term through the sale of a bond issue.

Bank-based corporate governance system

Organization of a supervisory board so that it is dominated by bankers and corporate insiders.

Bank collection float

The time that elapses between when a check is deposited into a bank account and when the funds are available to the depositor, during which period the bank is collecting payment from the payer's bank.

Bank discount basis

A convention used for quoting bids and offers for Treasury bills in terms of annualized yield, based on a 360-day year.

Bank draft

A draft addressed to a bank.

Banker's acceptance

A time draft under an irrevocable letter of credit confirmed by a prime U.S. bank presents relatively little risk of default. Also, some banks or other lenders may be willing to buy time drafts that a creditworthy foreign buyer has accepted or agreed to pay at a specified future date. In some cases, banks agree to accept the obligations of paying a draft, usually of a customer, for a fee; this is called a banker's acceptance.

Banker's Bank

A bank that is established by mutual consent by independent and unaffiliated banks to provide a clearinghouse for financial transactions.

Banker's Draft

Draft payable on demand and drawn by or on behalf of the bank itself; it is regarded as cash and cannot be returned unpaid.

Bank for International Settlements (BIS)

BIS, established in 1930, promotes cooperation among central banks in international financial settlements.

Members include: Australia, Austria, Belgium, Bulgaria, Canada, Czechoslovakia, Denmark, Finland, France, Germany, Greece, Hungary, Iceland, Ireland, Italy, Japan, Netherlands, Norway, Poland, Portugal, Romania, South Africa, Spain, Sweden, Switzerland, Turkey, the United Kingdom, the United States, and Yugoslavia. Bank headquarters are in Basle, Switzerland.

Bank Guarantee

An assurance, obtained from a bank by a foreign purchaser; that the bank will pay an exporter up to a given amount for goods shipped if the foreign purchaser defaults. See Letter of Credit.

Bank Holding Company

Any company which directly or indirectly owns or controls, with power to vote, more than five percent of voting shares of each of one or more other banks.

Bank Insurance Fund (BIF)

A unit of the Federal Deposit Insurance Corporation (FDIC) that provides deposit insurance for banks excluding thrifts.

Bank Investment Contract (BIC)

Interest guaranteed by the bank in a portfolio over a specific time frame with a specific yield.

Bank line

Line of credit that by a bank grants to a customer.

Bank Letter of Credit Policy

Standards allowing banks to confirm letters of credit by foreign banks supporting the purchase of US exports.

Bank note

A term used synonymously with paper money or currency issued by a bank. Notes are, in effect a promise to pay the bearer on demand the amount stated on the face of the note. Today, only the Federal Reserve Banks are authorized to issue bank notes, i.e. Federal Reserve notes, in the United States.

Bank of Central African States (BEAC)

The bank (French: Banque des Etats de l'Afrique Centrale, BEAC) issues a common currency unit, the Central African Franc. Members include The Cameroon, Central African Republic, Chad, People's Republic of Congo, Gabon, and Equitarial Guinea. France participates in management of the bank and provides guarantees for the currency. BEAC was established in April 1973; headquarters are in Yaoundé, Cameroon.

Bank Release

Negotiable time draft drawn on and accepted by a bank which adds its credit to that of an importer of merchandise.

Bank regulation

The formulationand issuance by authorized agencies of specific rules or regulations, under govering law, for the conduct and structure of banking.

Bank run (bank panic)

A series of unexpected cash withdrawals caused by a sudden decline in depositor confidence or fear that the bank will be closed by the chartering agency, i.e. many depositors withfraw cash almost simultaneously. Since the cash reserve a bank keeps on hand is only a small fraction of its depoits, a large number of withdrawals in a short period of time can deplete available cash and force the bank to close and possibly go out of business.

Bank trust department

Bank department that deals with estates, administers trusts, and provides services such as estate planning advice to its clients.

Bank wire

A computer message system linking major banks. It is used not for effecting payments, but as a mechanism to advise the receiving bank of some action that has occurred, e.g., the payment by a customer of funds into that bank's account.

Banker's acceptance

A short-term credit investment created by a nonfinancial firm and guaranteed by a bank as to payment. Acceptances are traded at discounts to face value in the secondary market. These instruments have been a popular investment for money market funds. They are commonly used in international transactions.

Banking Delay

Time required for processing and clearing a check through the banking system.

Bankmail

An agreement between a company engaged in a takeover bid and a bank that the bank will not finance the bid of another acquirer.

Bankruptcy

Inability to pay debts. In bankruptcy of a publicly owned entity, the ownership of the firm's assets is transferred from the stockholders to the bondholders.

Bankruptcy cost view

The argument that expected indirect and direct bankruptcy costs offset the other benefits from leverage so that the optimal amount of leverage is less than 100% debt financing.

Bankruptcy risk

The risk that a firm will be unable to meet its debt obligations. Also referred to as default or insolvency risk.

Bankruptcy view

The argument that expected bankruptcy costs preclude firms from financing entirely with debt.

Banque Arabe pour le Développement Economique en Afrique (BADEA)

See Arab Bank for Economic Development in Africa.

Banque Centrale des Etats de l'Afrique de l'Ouest (BECAO)

BECAO, which operates as a central bank under authority of the West African Monetary Union, issues the common currency for member states: Benin, Burkina Faso, Côte d'Ivoire, Mali, Niger, Senegal, and Togo.

Banque de Développement des Etats de l'Afrique Centrale (BDEAC)

See Central African States Development Bank.

Banque de Développement des Etats du Grand Lac (BDEGL)

See Development Bank of the Great Lakes States.

Banque des Etats de l'Afrique Centrale (BEAC)

See Bank of Central African States.

Banque Française du Commerce Extérieur (BFCE)

BFCE, a government-owned agency, is the French Government lender for officially supported export credits at preferential interest rates. The Bank, which provides financing for international trade, plays a coordinating role between exporters and the French government. BFCE services include:

(a) offering fixed-rate interim credit and payment plans during the manufacture of goods or performance of services;

(b) providing endorsements to gain access to refinancing and special low-interest loans and rediscounting the available portion of such credit with the Banque de France; and

(c) using funds borrowed in France and overseas under State guarantees to finance buyer credits running more than seven years as well as refinancing supplier credits for the same term. BFCE also manages Treasury guarantees on French overseas investment.

See Compagnie Française d'Assurance pour le Commerce Extérieur.

Banque Quest-Africaine de Développement (BOAD)

See West African Development Bank.

Bar

Slang for one million dollars.

Barbell strategy

A fixed income strategy in which the maturity's of the securities included in the portfolio are concentrated at two extremes.

Barefoot pilgrim

A slang term for an unsophisticated investor who has lost everything on the stock market.

Bargain hunter

In the context of general equities, purchaser who is extremely selective in the price sought on a transaction.

Bargaining Power

Each party negotiating to participate in an international business strategic alliance that can bring complementary skills and assets to the alliance which urgently needs them has real bargaining power. The goal in negotiations is to find ways for each partner to win short, medium and long term potential benefits thereby bringing forth its best creative powers, unique talent and significant advantages.

Bargain-purchase-price option

Gives the lessee the option to purchase the asset at a price below fair market value when the lease expires.

Barometer

Economic and market data that represent an overall trend. The Dow Jones Industrial Average is an example of a stock market barometer.

BARRA's performance analysis (PERFAN)

A method developed by BARRA, a consulting firm in Berkeley, Calif. It is commonly used by institutional investors applying performance attribution analysis to evaluate their money managers' performance.

Barrier options

Option contracts with trigger points that, when crossed, automatically generate buying or selling of other options. These are exotic options.

Barron's confidence index

Index measuring the ratio of the average yield on 10 top-grade bonds to the average yield on 10 intermediate-grade bonds. The discrepancy between high-rated top-grade bonds and low-rated bond yields establishes a measure that is indicative of investor confidence.

Barter

Barter is a one-time transaction bound under a single contract that specifies the direct exchange of selected goods or services for another of equivalent value. Barter is the oldest form of reciprocal trade. No financial transfers are involved in barter transactions. The time interval between exchanges is short and does not usually exceed 12 months. The limited flexibility of barter transactions makes these arrangements a rare occurrence in international commerce.

Base

A technical analysis tool. A chart pattern depicting the period when the supply and demand of a certain stock are in relative equilibrium, resulting in a narrow trading range. The merging of the support level and resistance level.

Base currency

Applies mainly to international equities. Currency in which gains or losses from operating an international portfolio are measured.

Base interest rate

Related: Benchmark interest rate.

Basel Convention

The Basel Convention restricts trade in hazardous waste, some non-hazardous wastes, solid wastes, and incinerator ash. It was adopted in 1989 by a United Nations-sponsored conference of 116 nations in Basel, Switzerland. Twenty nations must ratify the treaty before it goes into effect.

Base market value

A group of securities, average market price at a specific time. Used for the purpose of indexing.

Base period

A particular period of time used for comparative purposes when measuring economic data.

Base probability of loss

The probability of not achieving a portfolio expected return. Related: Value at risk.

Base rate

British equivalent of the US prime rate.

Basel Accord

Agreement concluded among country representatives in 1988 in Switzerland to develop standardized risk-based capital requirements for banks across countries.

Basic balance

In a balance of payments, the basic balance is the net balance of the combination of the current account and the capital account.

Basic business strategies

Key strategies a firm intends to pursue in carrying out its business plan.

Basic IRR rule

Accept the project if IRR is higher than the discount rate; reject the project if it is lower than the discount rate. It is wise to also consider net present value for project evaluation.

Basis

The price an investor pays for a security plus any out-of-pocket expenses. It is used to determine capital gains or losses for tax purposes when the stock is sold. Also, for a futures contract, the difference between the cash price and the futures price observed in the market.

Basis point

In the bond market, the smallest measure used for quoting yields is a basis point. Each percentage point of yield in bonds equals 100 basis points. Basis points also are used for interest rates. An interest rate of 5% is 50 basis points higher than an interest rate of 4.5%. Sometimes referred to as BPS, BIPS, and pronounced "Bips"

Basis price

Price expressed in terms of yield to maturity or annual rate of return.

Basis risk

Uncertainty about the basis at the time a hedge may be lifted. Hedging substitutes basis risk for price risk.

Basket

Applies to derivative products. Group of stocks that is formed with the intention of either being bought or sold all at once, usually to perform index arbitrage or a hedging program.

Basket options

Packages that involve the exchange of more than two currencies against a base currency at expiration. The basket option buyer purchases the right, but not the obligation, to receive designated currencies in exchange for a base currency, either at the prevailing foreign exchange market rate or at a prearranged rate of exchange. Multinational corporations with multicurrency cash flows frequently use basket options because it is generally cheaper to buy an option on a basket of currencies than to buy individual options on each of the currencies that make up the basket.

Basket trades

Related: Program trades.

BB

The two-character ISO 3166 country code for BARBADOS.

BBD

The ISO 4217 currency code for Barbadan Dollar.

BD

The two-character ISO 3166 country code for BANGLADESH.

BD form

An SEC required document of brokerage houses that outlines the firm's finances and officers.

BDS Statistic

A statistic based upon the correlation integral which examines the probability that a purely random system could have the same scaling properties as the system under study. See: Correlation Integral.

BDT

The ISO 4217 currency code for Bangladeshi Taka currency.

BE

The two-character ISO 3166 country code for BELGIUM.

BEACON (Boston Exchange Automated Communication Order-Routing Network)

This system permits the automatic execution of trades

based on the current stock prices on the consolidated markets at any of the US securities exchanges.

Bear

An investor who believes a stock or the overall market will decline. A bear market is a prolonged period of falling stock prices, usually by 20% or more. Related: bull.

Bear CD

A bear CD pays the holder a fraction of any fall in a given market index.

Bear hug

Often used in risk arbitrage. Hostile takeover attempt in which the acquirer offers an exceptionally large premium over the market value of the acquiree's share so as to as to squeeze (hug) the target into acceptance.

Bear market

Any market in which prices exhibit a declining trend. For a prolonged period, usually falling by 20% or more.

Bear raid

In the context of general equities, attempt by investors to move the price of a stock opportunistically by selling large numbers of shares short. The investors pocket the difference between the initial price and the new, lower price after this maneuver. This technique is illegal under SEC rules, which stipulate that every short sale must be on an uptick.

Bear spread

Applies to derivative products. Strategy in the options market designed to take advantage of a fall in the price of a security or commodity, usually executed by buying a combination of calls and puts on the same security at different strike prices in order to profit as the security's price falls.

Bear trap

The predicament facing short sellers when a bear market reverses its trend and becomes bullish. The assets continue to sell in anticipation of further declines in price, and short sellers then are forced to cover at higher prices.

Bearer bond

Bonds that are not registered on the books of the issuer. Such bonds are held in physical form by the owner, who receives interest payments by physically detaching coupons from the bond certificate and delivering them to the paying agent.

Bearer form

Describes issue form of security not registered on the issuing corporation's books, and therefore payable to its bearer. See also: Bearer bond; coupon bond.

Bearer share

Security not registered on the books of the issuing corporation and thus payable to possessor of the shares. Negotiable without endorsement and transferred by delivery, thus avoiding some of the control associated with ordinary shares. Dividends are payable upon presentation of dividend coupons, which are dated or numbered. Applies mainly to international equities.

Bearish

Words used to describe investor attitude.

Beating the gun

In the context of general equities, gaining an advantageous price in a trade through a quick response to market developments.

BEF

The ISO 4217 currency code for Belgium Franc.

Before-tax contributions

The portion of an employee's salary contributed to a retirement plan before federal income taxes are deducted; this reduces the individual's gross income for federal tax purposes.

Before-tax profit margin

The ratio of net income before taxes to net sales.

Beggar-thy-neighbor

An international trade policy of competitive devaluations and increased protective barriers that one country institutes to gain at the expense of its trading partners.

Beggar-thy-neighbor devaluation

A devaluation that is designed to cheapen a nation's currency and thereby increase its exports at the expense of other countries. Devaluation can also reduce a nation's imports. Such devaluations often lead to trade wars.

Behind

Used for listed equity securities. At the same price but entered after your order/interest, such as on the specialist's book. Antithesis of ahead of you.

Belgium-Luxembourg Economic Union (BLEU)

BLEU (French: UEBL, from Union Economique Belgo-Luxembourgeoise), established in July 1921, introduced a system of monetary association between Belgium and Luxembourg.

Bell

Signal on a stock exchange to indicate the open and close of trading.

Bellwether issues

Related: Benchmark issues.

Below par

Less than the nominal or face value of a security.

BEM

See under Big Emerging Markets.

Benchmark

The performance of a predetermined set of securities, used for comparison purposes. Such sets may be based on published indexes or may be customized to suit an investment strategy.

Beneficiary

The person in whose favor a draft is issued or a letter of credit opened.

Benelux Economic Union

Benelux (acronym for Belgium, Netherlands, and Luxembourg) is an economic union originally established in January 1948 and revised in January 1960. Benelux continues as an internal regional association within the European Community (EC) because the association's aims do not conflict with EC goals.

Benchmark error

Use of an inappropriate proxy for the true market portfolio.

Benchmark interest rate

Also called the base interest rate, it is the minimum interest rate investors will demand for investing in a non-Treasury security. It is also tied to the yield to maturity offered on the comparable-maturity Treasury security that was most recently issued (on-the-run).

Benchmark issue

Also called on-the-run or current-coupon issue or bellwether issues. In the secondary market, the benchmark issue is the most recently auctioned Treasury issues for each maturity.

Beneath

Used for listed equity securities. 1) Behind; 2) Lower in price.

Beneficial Owner

As used for most purposes under the federal securities laws. A beneficial owner of stock is any person or entity with sole or shared power to vote or dispose of the stock. This SEC definition is intended to include a holder who enjoys the benefits of ownership although the shares may be held in another name.

Beneficial ownership

Often used in risk arbitrage. Person who enjoys the benefits of ownership even though title is in another name. (Abused through the illegal use of a parking violation.)

Beneficiary

Term used to refer to the person who receives the benefits of a trust or the recipient of the proceeds of a life insurance policy.

Bequest

Property left to an heir under the terms of a will.

Best's rating

A rating A.M. Best Co. assigns to insurance companies based on the company's ability to meet its obligations to its policyholders.

Best-efforts sale

A method of securities distribution/underwriting in which the securities firm agrees to sell as much of the offering as possible and return any unsold shares to the issuer. As opposed to a guaranteed or fixed-price sale, in which the underwriter agrees to sell a specific number of shares (and holds any unsold shares in its own account if necessary).

Best Information Available

Under GATT rules, when a respondent in an anti-dumping or countervailing duty case either declines to provide information, or provides inadequate information, the investigating authority has the right to resort to other information, a practice known as best information available. Determinations of BIA may be made on a case-by-case basis; in some cases, it may be information submitted be petitioners.

Best-interests-of-creditors test

The requirement that a claim holder voting against a plan of reorganization must receive at least as much as if the debtor were liquidated.

Beta

The measure of an asset's risk in relation to the market (for example, the S&P500) or to an alternative benchmark or factors. Roughly speaking, a security with a beta of 1.5, will have move, on average, 1.5 times the market return. [More precisely, that stock's excess return (over and above a short-term money market rate) is expected to move 1.5 times the market excess return).] According to asset pricing theory, beta represents the type of risk, systematic risk, that cannot be diversified away. When using beta, there are a number of issues that you need to be aware of: (1) betas may change through time; (2) betas may be different depending on the direction of the market (i.e. betas may be greater for down moves in the market rather than up moves); (3) the estimated beta will be biased if the security does not frequently trade; (4) the beta is not necessarily a complete measure of risk (you may need multiple betas). Also, note that the beta is a measure of comovement, not volatility. It is possible for a security to have a zero beta and higher volatility than the market.

Beta equation (security)

The market beta of a security is determined as follows: Regress excess returns of stock y on excess returns of the market. The slope coefficient is beta. Define n as number of observation numbers.

Beta=

[(n) (sum of [xy])]-[(sum of x) (sum of y)]/

[(n) (sum of [xx])]-[(sum of x) (sum of x)]

where: n = # of observations (usually 36 to 60 months)

x = rate of return for the S&P 500 index

y = rate of return for the security.

Related: Alpha

BF

The two-character ISO 3166 country code for BURKINA FASO.

BG

The two-character ISO 3166 country code for BULGARIA.

BGL

The ISO 4217 currency code for Bulgarian Lev.

BH

The two-character ISO 3166 country code for BAHRAIN.

BHD

The ISO 4217 currency code for Bahrainian Dinar.

BI

The two-character ISO 3166 country code for BURUNDI.

Biased expectations theories

Related: Pure expectations theory.

Bid

The price a potential buyer is willing to pay for a security. Sometimes also used in the context of takeovers where one corporation is bidding for (trying to buy) another corporation. In trading, we have the bid-ask spread which is the difference between what buyers are willing to pay and what sellers are asking for in terms of price.

Bid away

Refers to over-the-counter trading. Bid from another dealer exists at the same (listed) or higher (OTC) price.

Bid-asked spread

The difference between the bid and the asked prices.

Bidder

Any person, company who offers a bid.

Bidder list

A list maintained by an organization giving names and addresses of suppliers of various goods and services from whom bids and proposals can be solicited.

Bid price

This is the quoted bid, or the highest price an investor is willing to pay to buy a security. Practically speaking, this is the available price at which an investor can sell shares of stock. Related: Ask, offer.

Bid-to-cover ratio

The ratio of the number of bids received in a Treasury security auction compared to the number of accepted bids.

Bid wanted

Used in the context of general equities. Announcement that a holder of securities wants to sell and will entertain bids.

Bidder

A firm or person that wants to buy a firm or security.

Bidding buyer

In the context of general equities, a nonaggressive buyer who prefers to await a natural seller in the hope of paying a lower price.

Bidding through the market

In the context of general equities, aggressive willingness to purchase a security at a premium to the inside market. Contrast with bidding buyer.

Bidding up

Moving the bid price higher.

BIF

(1) See: Bank Insurance Fund. (2) The ISO 4217 currency code for Burundian Franc.

Bifurcation

When a non-linear dynamic system develops twice the possible solutions that it had before it passed its critical level. A bifurcation cascade is often called the period doubling route to chaos because the transition from an orderly system to a chaotic system often occurs when the number of possible solutions begins increasing, doubling each time.

Bifurcation Diagram

A graph that shows the critical points where bifurcation occurs, and the possible solutions that exist at that point.

Big Bang

The term applied to the liberalization in 1986 of the London Stock Exchange (LSE) when trading was automated.

Big Board

A nickname for the New York Stock Exchange (NYSE). Also known as The Exchange. More than 2,000 common and preferred stocks are traded. Founded in 1792, the NYSE is the oldest exchange in the United States, and the largest. It is located on Wall Street in New York City.

Big Emerging Markets (BEM

A group of fast-growing economies that the Department of Commerce has identified as major U.S. export markets in the future: Argentina, Brazil, the Chinese Economic Area (China, Hong Kong, and Taiwan), India, Indonesia, Mexico, Poland, South Africa, South Korea, and Turkey. In 1994, the total population of the BEMs was 2.8 billion, about half of world population. Market demand on the part of the BEMs is growing rapidly. Between 1990 and 1995, Big Emerging Market nation's imports surged, garnering 30 percent of the world's import share in 1995 compared to 22 percent in 1990. The BEM countries accounted for 44 percent of the dollar growth in world imports between 1990 and 1995. (U.S. Department of Commerce)

Big picture

To highlight trading interest due to the size of the trade.

Big producer

A successful broker who generates a large volume of commission. See Rainmaker.

Big uglies

Unpopular stocks.

Bilateral Clearing Agreement

Government-to-government reciprocal trade arrangement whereby two nations agree to a trade turnover of specified value over one or more years. The value of the products traded under the agreement is denominated in accounting units expressed in major currencies—such as clearing U.S. dollars, clearing Swiss francs, etc. Exporters in each country are paid by designated local banks in domestic currencies.

Bilateral Investment Treaty (BIT)

A bilateral investment treaty, BIT, ensures U.S. investments abroad of national or most favored nation treatment; prohibits the imposition of performance requirements; and allows the American investor to engage top management in a foreign country without regard to nationality. BITs ensure the right to make investment-related transfers, and guarantee that expropriation takes place only in accordance with accepted international law. BITs also guarantee access by an investing party to impar ti al and binding international arbitration for dispute settlement.

Bilateral Steel Agreements (BSA)

The U.S. negotiated ten bilateral steel agreements, BSAs, with major steel trading partners. Under BSAs, the governments agreed to reduce or eliminate state intervention — that is, domestic subsidies and market barriers.

Billing cycle

The time elapsed between billing periods for goods sold or services rendered.

Bill of exchange

A signed, written order by one business that instructs another business to pay a third business a specific amount. See also draft.

Bill of Lading

Bills of lading are contracts between the owner of the goods and the carrier. There are two types. A straight bill of lading is nonnegotiable. A negotiable or shipper's order bill of lading can be bought, sold, or traded while goods are in transit and is used for many types of financing transactions. The customer usually needs the original or a copy as proof of ownership to take possession of the goods.

Binational Commission (BNC)

U.S.-Mexico commission which provides a forum to further promote closer economic and commercial ties between the U.S. and Mexico.

Binder

An amount of money paid to indicate good faith in a transaction before the transaction is completed.

Binomial option pricing model

An option pricing model in which the underlying asset can assume one of only two possible, discrete values in the next time period for each value that it can take on in the preceding time period.

Biological Agents

Several classes of biological agents have been identified according to their degree of pathogenic hazard, and are controlled by the United States in accord with provisions of the Australia Group. Applications submitted to the Department of Commerce for the export of certain biological agents are generally referred to the Department of State and the intelligence community on a case-by-case basis.

BIPS

See: Basis point.

BIS

See: Bank for International Settlements.

Bi-weekly mortgage loan

A mortgage loan on which interest and principal payments are made every half-month (total of 26 payments) as opposed to monthly payments. This results in earlier loan retirement.

BJ

The two-character ISO 3166 country code for BENIN.

Black Friday

A precipitous drop in a financial market . The original Black Friday occurred on September 24, 1869, when prospectors attempted to corner the gold market.

Black market

An illegal market.

Black Monday

Refers to October 19, 1987, when the Dow Jones Industrial Average fell 508 points on the heels of sharp drops the previous week. On Monday, October 27, 1997, the Dow dropped 554 points. While the point drop set a new record, the percentage decline was substantially less than in 1987.

Black-Scholes option-pricing model

A model for pricing call options based on arbitrage arguments. Uses the stock price, the exercise price, the risk-free interest rate, the time to expiration, and the expected standard deviation of the stock return. Developed by Fischer Black and Myron Scholes in 1973.

Blank check

A check that is duly signed, but the amount of the check is left blank to be supplied by the drawee.

Blank check offering

An initial public offering by a company whose business activities are undefined and therefore peculative.

Blank Check Preferred Stock

This is stock over which the board of directors has broad authority to determine voting, dividend, conversion, and other rights. While it can be used to enable a company to meet changing financial needs, its most important use is to implement poison pills or to prevent takeover by placement of this stock with friendly investors.

Blanket certification form

See: NASD form FR-1.

Blanket fidelity bond

SEC-required insurance coverage that brokerage firms are required to have in order to cover fraudulent trading by employees.

Blanket inventory lien

A secured loan that gives the lender a lien against all the borrower's inventories.

Blanket Mortgage

A mortgage that covers at least two pieces of real estate as collateral for the same mortgage.

Blanket Order

See open-end contract.

Blanket recommendation

A recommendation by a brokerage firm sent to all its customers advising that they buy or sell a particular stock regardless of investment objectives or portfolio size.

Blind pool

A limited partnership that does not announce its intentions as to what properties will be acquired.

Blind trust

A trust in which a fiduciary third party has total discretion to make investments on behalf of a beneficiary while the beneficiary is uninformed about the holdings of the trust.

Blitzkrieg tender offer

In the context of a takeover, refers to a tender offer that is priced so attractively that the tender is completed quickly.

Block

Large quantity of stock or large dollar amount of bonds held or traded. As a rule of thumb, 10,000 shares or more of stock and $200,000 or more worth of bonds would be described as a block.

Block call

In the context of general equities, conference meeting during which customer indications and orders, along with the traders' own buy/sell preferences, are conveyed to the entire organization. See block list.

Blocked Currency

Currency that cannot be freely transferred into convertible currencies and expatriated. Usually synonymous with foreign-owned funds or earnings in countries where government exchange regulations prohibit their expatriation.

Block house

Brokerage firms that help to find potential buyers or sellers of large block trades.

Block list

In the context of general equities, listing of stock the investment bank is looking for (wants to buy) or (wants to sell) at the beginning of the day, whether on an agency or principal basis.

Block trade

A large trading order, defined on the New York Stock Exchange as an order that consists of 10,000 shares of a given stock or at a total market value of $200,000 or more.

Block trader

A dealer who will take a position in the block trades to accommodate customer buyers and sellers of blocks. See: Dealer, market maker, principal.

Block voting

Describes a group of shareholders banding together to vote their shares in a single block.

Blocked currency

A currency that is not freely convertible to other currencies due to exchange controls.

Blocked funds

Cash flows generated by a foreign project that cannot be immediately repatriated to the parent firm because of capital flow restrictions imposed by the host government.

Blow-off top

A steep and rapid increase in price followed by a steep and rapid drop. This is an indicator seen in charts and used in technical analysis of stock price and market trends.

Blowout

The rapid sale of all shares in a new securities offering. See: hot issue.

Blue list

Daily financial publication featuring bonds offered for sale by dealers and banks that represent billions of dollars in par value. Also available on-line at www.bluelist.com.

Blue-chip company

Used in the context of general equities. Large and creditworthy company. Company renowned for the quality and wide acceptance of its products or services,and for its ability to make money and pay dividends. Gilt-edged security.

Blue chip stocks

Common stock of well-known companies with a history of growth and dividend payments.

Blue Lantern

Blue Lantern, a procedure pertaining to U.S. Munitions List items, is intended to verify that information stated on export license applications is valid and that the use of the commodity or service exported is consistent with the terms of the license. It includes prelicense and postshipment checks of export applications conducted by designated officials at U.S. embassies. Blue Lantern was initiated in September 1990 by the State Department's Office of Defense Trade Controls.

Blue-sky laws

State laws covering the issue and trading of securities.

BM

The two-character ISO 3166 country code for BERMUDA.

BMD

The ISO 4217 currency code for Bermudan Dollar.

BN

The two-character ISO 3166 country code for BRUNEI DARUSSALAM.

BNC

See under Binational Commission.

BND

The ISO 4217 currency code for Brunei Darussalam Dollar.

BO

The two-character ISO 3166 country code for BOLIVIA.

BOB

The ISO 4217 currency code for Bolivian Boliviano.

Bo Derek stock

High quality stock.

Board broker

Employee of the Chicago Board Options Exchange who manages away from the market orders, which cannot be executed immediately.

Board of Directors

Individuals elected by the shareholders of a corporation who carry out certain tasks established in the charter.

Board of Governors of the Federal Reserve System

The managing body of the Federal Reserve System, set which policies on bank practices and the money supply.

Board room

A room at a brokerage firm where its clients can watch an electronic board displaying stock prices and transactions. Also refers to the room where Board of Directors meetings take place.

Bogey

The return an investment manager is compared to for performance evaluation.

Boiler room

Used to describe place or operation in which unscrupulous salespeople call and try to sell people speculative, even fraudulent, securities.

Boilerplate

Standard terms and conditions.

Bollinger Bands

Plus or minus two standard deviations where the standard deviations are calculated historically in a moving window estimation. Hence, the bands will widen if the most recent data is more volatile. If the prices break out of the band, this is considered a significant move.

Bolsa

Spanish for stock exchange.

Bolsa de Commercio de Santiago (SSE)

Chile's preeminent stock exchange.

Bolsa de Valores de Rio de Janeiro (BVRJ)

Brazil's second-largest stock exchange.

Bolsa de Valores de Sao Paulo (BOVESPA)

The largest stock exchange in Brazil.

Bolt

Used for listed equity securities. Block trading version of COLT.

Bombay Stock Exchange (BSE)

See: National Stock Exchange; Mumbai stock exchange.

Bond

Bonds are debt and are issued for a period of more than one year. The US government, local governments, water districts, companies and many other types of institutions sell bonds. When an investor buys bonds, he or she is lending money. The seller of the bond agrees to repay the principal amount of the loan at a specified time. Interest-bearing bonds pay interest periodically.

Bond (performance)

A bond executed in connection with a contract that secures the performance and fulfillment of all conditions and terms written into the purchase order.

Bond agreement

A contract for privately placed debt.

Bond anticipation note (BAN)

A short-term debt instrument issued by a state or municipality to borrow against the proceeds of an upcoming bond issue.

Bond broker

A broker on the floor of an exchange who trades bonds.

Bond Buyer

A daily publication featuring many essential statistics and index figures relevant to the fixed income markets.

Bond Buyer's municipal bond index

A municipal bond price tracking index published daily by the Bond Buyer.

Bond counsel

An attorney who prepares the legal opinion concerning a municipal bond issue.

Bond covenant

A contractual provision in a bond indenture. A positive covenant requires certain actions, and a negative covenant limits certain actions.

Bond crowd

Members of the stock exchange who transact bond orders on the floor of the exchange.

Bond discount

The difference by which a bond's market price is lower than its face value. The antithesis of a bond premium, which prevails when the market price of a bond is higher than its face value. See: Original issue discount.

Bonded Exchange

Exchange which cannot be freely converted into other currencies.

Bonded Warehouse

A building authorized by Customs authorities for storage of goods on which payment of duties is deferred until the goods are removed.

Bond-equivalent basis

The method used for computing the bond-equivalent yield.

Bond equivalent yield

Bond yield calculated on an annual percentage rate method. Differs from annual effective yield.

Bond fund

A mutual fund that emphasizes income—consistent with risk, rather than growth—by investing in corporate, municipal, or US government debt obligations, or some combination of them.

Bond indenture

Contract that sets forth the promises of a corporate bond issuer and the rights of investors.

Bond indexing

Designing a bond portfolio so that its performance will match the performance of some bond index.

Bond market association

An international trade association of broker/dealers and banks in US government and federal agency securities, municipal securities, mortgage-backed securities, and money market securities.

Bond mutual fund

A mutual fund holding bonds.

Bond of Indemnity

An insurance policy that indemnifies the corporation, the shareholder and the Transfer Agent against any and all claims arising from the replacement by the Transfer Agent of certificates lost or stolen.

Bond points

A conventional unit of measure for bond prices set at $1 and equivalent to 1% of the $100 face value of the bond. A price of 80 means that the bond is selling at 80% of its face or par value.

Bond power

A form used in the transfer of registered bonds from one owner to a different owner.

Bond premium

See: Bond discount

Bond rating

A rating based on the possibility of default by a bond issuer. The ratings range from AAA (highly unlikely to default) to D (in default). See: Rating, investment grade.

Bond ratio

The percentage of a company's capitalization represented by bonds. The ratio is calculated by dividing the total bonds due after one year by that same figure plus all other equity. See: Debt-to-equity-ratio.

Bond swap

The sale of one bond issue and purchase of another bond issue simultaneously. See: Swap; swap order.

Bond value

With respect to convertible bonds, the value the security would have if it were not convertible. That is the market value of the bond minus the value of the conversion option.

Bondholder

The firm often has stockholders and bondholders. In a liquidation, the bondholders have first priority.

BONDPAR

A system that monitors and evaluates the performance of a fixed income portfolio, as well as the individual securities held in the portfolio. BONDPAR decomposes the return into the elements beyond the manager's control—such as the interest rate environment and client-imposed duration policy constraints—and those that the management process contributes to, such as interest rate management, sector/quality allocations, and individual bond selection.

Bonds Enabling Annual Retirement Savings (BEARS)

Holders of BEARS receive the face value of bonds underlying call option, which are exercised by CUBS (an acronym for Calls Underwritten by Swanbrook). If the calls are exercised by CUBS, BEARS holders receive the total of the exercise price.

Bond System

The Bond System, a part of Customs' Automated Commercial System, provides information on bond coverage. A Customs bond is a contract between a principal, usually an importers, and a surety which is obtained to insure performance of an obligation imposed by law or regulation. The bond covers potential loss of duties, taxes, and penalties for specific types of transactions. Customs is the contract beneficiary.

Bon voyage bonus

See: Greenmail.

Boning

Charging a lot more for an asset than its worth.

Book

A banker or trader's positions.

Book cash

A firm's cash balance as reported in its financial statements. Also called ledger cash.

Book profit

The cumulative book income plus any gain or loss on disposition of assets.

Book runner

The managing underwriter for a new issue. The book runner maintains the book of securities sold.

Book to bill

The book-to-bill ratio is the ratio of orders taken (booked) to products shipped and bills sent (billed). The ratio measures whether the company has more orders than it can deliver (>1), equal amounts (=1), or less (<1). This ratio is of significant interest to investors/ traders in the high-technology sector.

Book-to-bill ratio

A measure of sales trends of a company or industry. A number above 1 indicates an expanding market, and a number below 1 is a contracting market. For example, a book-to-bill ratio of 1.03 means that for every $100 of products shipped, $103 in new orders was received.

Book to market

The ratio of book value to market value of equity. A high ratio means is often interpreted as a value stock (the market is valuing equity relatively cheaply compared to book value). This is the same as a low price-to-book value ratio. Value managers often form portfolios of securities with high book to market values.

Book value

The difference between a company's assets and its liabilities, usually expressed in per-share terms. It takes into account all money invested in the company since its founding, as well as retained earnings. It is calculated by substracting liabilities from assets and dividing the result by the number of shares outstanding. Comparing book value to share price is one way to gauge if a company' stock is undervalued or overvalued.

Book value per share

The ratio of stockholder equity to the average number of common shares. Book value per share should not be thought of as an indicator of economic worth, since it reflects accounting valuation (and not necessarily market valuation).

Book-Entry

Registered ownership of stock without the issuance of a corresponding stock certificate, as is the case with dividend reinvestment and direct purchase plans, employee plans and Direct Registration System issuances. Periodic statements of ownership are issued instead of certificates.

Book-entry securities

System in which securities are not represented by paper certificates but are maintained in computerized records at the Fed in the names of member banks, which in turn keep computer records of the securities they own as well as those they are holding for customers. In the case of other securities where a book-entry has developed, certificates reside in a central clearinghouse or by another agent. These securities do not move from holder to holder.

Bootstrap

Term used to describe the start-up of a company with very little capital.

Bootstrapping

Creating a theoretical spot rate curve using one yield projection as the basis for the yield of the next maturity.

Border Cargo Selectivity (BCS)

BCS is an automated cargo selectivity system based on historical and other information. The system is designed to facilitate cargo processing and to improve Customs enforcement capabilities by providing targeting information to border locations. The system is used for the land-border environment.

Border Environment Cooperation Commission (BECC)

The BECC is a U.S.-Mexican binational commission intended to facilitate border environmental clean-up and to provide additional support for community adjustment and investment related to the North American Free Trade Agreement. The BECC will assist border states and local communities in coordinating, designing, and financing environmental infrastructure projects with cross-border impact. To be eligible, projects must observe the environmental laws for the place where the project is located or carried out. The BECC will certify projects to the North American Development Bank (NADBank) and will seek to mobilize financing from the NADBank, federal, state, and local grants, loans, and guarantees, and the private sector. See North American Development Bank.

Borrow

To obtain or receive money on loan with the promise or understanding that it will be repaid.

Borrowed reserves

Funds borrowed from a Federal Reserve Bank by member banks to maintain the required reserve ratios.

Borrower fallout

In the mortgage pipeline, the risk that prospective borrowers of loans committed to be closed will elect to withdraw from the contract.

BOT

See Build-Operate-Transfer.

Bot

Shorthand for bought. Antithesis of SL, meaning sold.

Bottom

Refers to the base support level for market prices of any type. Also used in the context of securities to refer to the lowest market price of a security during a specific time-frame.

Bottom fisher

An investor seeking stocks that have fallen to prices at or near their bottom, which he or she believes will trend up in the future.

Bottom line

Accounting term for the net profit or loss.

Bottomline growth

Growth in net profit. Also see topline growth.

Bottom-up equity management style

A management style that de-emphasizes the significance of economic and market cycles, focusing instead on the analysis of individual stocks.

Bought deal

Security issue in which one or two underwriters buy the entire issue.

Bounce

A check returned by a bank because it is not payable, usually because of insufficient funds. Also used in the context of securities to refer to the rejection and ensuing reclamation of a security; a stock price's abrupt decline and recovery.

Boundaryless Organization

A business organization that eliminates inefficient boundaries between organizational levels and functions of its workers; a supplier which enters into alliances to better serve its customers; an information system that has connections to any country in the world—are examples of the strong trend toward future flexible operations for better growth potential.

Bourse

French for a stock market.

Boutique

A small, specialized brokerage firm that offers limited services and products to a limited number of clients. Antithesis of financial supermarket.

Box

The actual physical location at a brokerage house or bank where securities or other documents are stored for safekeeping. Alternatively, a quotation machine or battery march.

Box spread

A type of option arbitrage in which both a bull spread and a bear spread are established for a near-riskless position. One spread is established using put options and the other is established using calls. The spread may both be debit spreads (call bull spread vs. put bear spread) or both credit spreads (call bear spread vs. put bull spread). Break-Even Point—the stock price (or prices) at which a particular strategy neither makes nor loses money. It generally pertains to the result at the expiration date of the options involved in the strategy. A "dynamic" break-even point is one that changes as time passes.

BR

The two-character ISO 3166 country code for BRAZIL.

Bracket

A term signifying the extent of an underwriter's commitment in a new issue, e.g., major bracket or minor bracket.

Bracket creep

The gradual movement into higher tax brackets when incomes increase as a result of inflation.

Brady bonds

Bonds issued by emerging countries under a debt reduction plan.

Branch

An operation in a foreign country incorporated in the home country.

Brand Name Specification

A specification that cites a brand name, model name, model number or some other designation that identifies a specific product as an example of the desired quality of merchandise.

Breadth

The percentage of assets or stocks advancing relative to those unchanged or declining. Also the number of independent forecasts available per year. A stock picker forecasting returns to 100 stocks every quarter exhibits a breadth of 400, assuming each forecast is independent (based on separate information).

Breadth of the market

In the context of general equities, percentage of stocks participating in a particular market move. Technical analysts say there was significant breadth if two-thirds of the stocks listed on an exchange move in the same direction during a trading session. See: A/D line.

Break

A rapid and sharp price decline. Related: Crash.

Break Bulk

Loose cargo, such as cartons, stowed directly in the ship's hold as opposed to containerized or bulk cargo. See "Containerization."

Break price

Used in the context of general equities. Change one's offering or bid prices to move to a more realistic, tight level where execution is more feasible. Often done to trim one's position, thus "breaking price" from where the trades occurred (if long, "break price" downward 1/8 a point or more).

Break-even analysis

An analysis of the level of sales at which a project would make zero profit.

Break-even lease payment

The lease payment at which a party to a prospective lease is indifferent between entering and not entering into a lease arrangement.

Break-even payment rate

The prepayment rate of an MBS coupon that will produce the same cash flow yield (CFY) as that of a predetermined benchmark MBS coupon. Used to identify for coupons higher than the benchmark coupon the prepayment rate that will produce the same cash flow yield (CFY) as that of the benchmark coupon; and for coupons lower than the benchmark coupon the lowest prepayment rate that will do so.

Break-even point

Refers to the price at which a transaction produces neither a gain nor a loss. In the context of options, the term has the additional definitions:

1. Long calls and short uncovered calls: strike price plus premium.
2. Long puts and short uncovered puts: strike price minus premium.
3. Short covered call: purchase price minus premium.
4. Short put covered by short stock: short sale price of underlying stock plus premium.

Break-even tax rate

The tax rate at which a party to a prospective transaction is indifferent between entering into and not entering into the transaction.

Break-even time

Related: Premium payback period.

Breaking the syndicate

Terminating an agreement among underwriters, specifically the investment banking group assembled to underwrite the issue of a security.

Breakout

A rise in a security's price above a resistance level (commonly its previous high price) or a drop below a level of support (commonly the former lowest price.) A breakout is taken to signify a continuing move in the same direction. Can be used by technical analysts as a buy or sell indicator.

Breakpoint sale

For mutual funds, refers to the investment amount necessary to make the fundholder eligible for a reduced sales charge. See: Letter of intent; right of accumulation.

Breakup value

See: Private market value.

Breeden, Douglas T.

Inventor of one of the foundational asset pricing models in finance, the consumption based capital asset pricing model. Chairman of Smith Breeden Associates.

Bretton Woods Agreement

An agreement signed by the original United Nations members in 1944 that established the International

Monetary Fund (IMF) and the post-World War II international monetary system of fixed exchange rates.

Bridge financing

Interim financing of one sort or another used to solidify a position until more permanent financing is arranged.

"Bring it out"

In the context of general equities, "make stock available for sale to indicated buyers."

British clearers

The large clearing banks that dominate deposit taking and short-term lending in the domestic sterling market.

British High Commission (BHC)

The term British High Commission (BHC, or High Commission, HC, or Her Majesty's High Commission, HMHC) is used in lieu of "embassy" in Commonwealth countries.

British Overseas Trade Board (BOTB)

The BOTB, located in the Department of Trade and Industry (DTI), advises on international trade and guides the government's export promotion program, including policy, financing, and overseas projects. The Board is composed of industry and government representatives; the chairman is an industrialist, the Chief Executive is a member of DTI. The export departments of the BOTB's regional offices work together with commercial staff from the Foreign and Commonwealth Office (FCO) to provide commercial assistance through UK overseas offices.

BRL

The ISO 4217 currency code for Brazilian Real.

Broad-Base

Generally referring to an index, it indicates that the index is composed of a sufficient number of stocks or of stocks in a variety of industry groups. See also: Narrow-Based.

Broad Market

Usually refers to indices such as the Wilshire 5000 that track the performance of 5,000 securities, rather than the more narrow measures such as the Dow Jones Industrial Average and the S and P 500.

Broad tape

An expanded version of the ticker tape, which is displayed on a screen in the board room of a brokerage firm and shows constantly updated financial information and news.

Broken up

Used for listed equity securities. Prevented from executing a trade (committed to upstairs) due to exchange priority rules excluding one's order (e.g., higher bid/lower offer on floor, market order to satisfy).

Broker

An individual who is paid a commission for executing customer orders. Either a floor broker who executes orders on the floor of the exchange, or an upstairs broker who handles retail customers and their orders. Also, person who acts as an intermediary between a buyer and seller, usually charging a commission. A "broker" who specializes in stocks, bonds, commodities, or options acts as an agent and must be registered with the exchange where the securities are traded. Antithesis of dealer.

Broker-dealer

Any person, other than a bank, engaged in the business of buying or selling securities on its own behalf or for others. See: Dealer.

Broker loan rate

Related: Call money rate.

Brokered CD

A certificate of deposit issued by a bank or thrift institution bought by a brokerage firm in bulk for the purpose of reselling to brokerage customers. A broker CD features a higher interest rate, usually 1% higher, and is FDIC insured and do not usually have commissions.

Brokered market

A market in which an intermediary offers search services to buyers and sellers.

Brokers' loans

Money brorowed by brokers from banks for uses such as financing specialists's inventories of stock, financing the underwriting of new issues of corporate and municipal securities, and financing customer margin accounts.

Brought over the wall

Compelling a research analyst of an investment bank to work in the underwriting department for a corporate client, therefore allowing for the transmission of insider information. Also called "Over the Chinese wall".

Brussels Stock Exchange (BSE)

Stock exchange that handles the majority of securities transactions in Belgium.

Brussels Tariff Nomenclature

A once widely used international tariff classification system which preceded the Customs Cooperation

Council Nomenclature (CCCN) and the Harmonized System Nomenclature (HS). The BTN was changed in name only to the CCCN in 1976 to avoid confusion with the tariff of the European Community.

BS

The two-character ISO 3166 country code for BAHAMAS.

BSD

The ISO 4217 currency code for Bahamas Dollar.

BT

The two-character ISO 3166 country code for BHUTAN.

BTM

See: Book to market.

BTN

The ISO 4217 currency code for Bhutan Ngultrum.

Bubble theory

Security prices sometimes move wildly above their true values, or the price falls sharply until the "bubble bursts.".

Budget

A detailed schedule of financial activity, such as an advertising budget, a sales budget, or a capital budget.

Budget authority

Broad responsibility by Congress that government agencies have the power to spend federal funds. Congress can specify criteria for the spending of these funds. For example, it may stipulate that a given agency must spend within a specific year, number of years, or any time in the future.

The basic forms of budget authority are; appropriations, authority to borrow, contract authority, and authority to obligate and expend offsetting receipts and collections. The period of time during which Congress makes funds available may be specified as one-year, multiple years or no year. The available amount may be classified as either definite or indefinite; a specific amount or an unspecified amount can be made available. Authority may also be classified as current or permanent. Permanent authority requires no current action by Congress.

Budget deficit

The amount by which government spending exceeds government revenues.

Buck

Slang for one million dollars.

Bucket shop

An illegal brokerage firm that accepts customer orders but does not attain immediate executions. A bucket shop broker promises the customer a certain price, but waits until a price discrepancy is present and the trade is advantageous to the firm and then keeps the difference as profit. Alternatively, the broker may never fill the customer's order but keep the money.

Budapest Stock Exchange

Established in 1864, the major securities market of Hungary.

Budget surplus

The amount by which government revenues exceed government pending.

Buenos Aires Stock Exchange (Bolsa de Comercio de Buenos Aires)

Argentina's major securities market.

Build a book

In the context of general equities, develop customer orders to gather demand/supply in order to make a bid or an offer.

Builder buydown loan

A mortgage loan on newly developed property that the builder subsidizes during the early years of the development. The builder uses cash to buy down the mortgage rate to a lower level than the prevailing market loan rate for some period of time. The typical buydown is 3% of the interest rate amount for the first year, 2% for the second year, and 1% for the third year (also referred to as a 3-2-1 buydown).

Build-Operate-Transfer (BOT)

Debt and equity financing of a major turnkey project, such as a nuclear power plant. The foreign supplier constructs and then operates the completed plant for profit over a contracted number of years. Until the plant is transferred to local ownership, the revenues derived from its operations serve to service debt and generate returns for the supplier.

Bulge

A short-lived stock price increase. Synonymous with bubble.

Bulge bracket

A tier of firms in an underwriting syndicate that have the highest participation level. See: Mezzanine bracket.

Bulk Cargo

Bulk cargo is unbound as loaded and carried aboard ship; it is without mark or count, in a loose unpackaged form, and has homogeneous characteristics.

Bulk Shipments

Shipments which are not packaged, but are loaded directly into the vessel's holds. Examples of commodities that can be shipped in bulk are ores, coal, scrap, iron, grain, rice, vegetable oil, tallow, fuel oil, fertilizers, and similar commodities.

Bull

An investor who thinks the market will rise. Related: Bear.

Bull-bear bond

Bond whose principal repayment is linked to the price of another security. The bonds are issued in two tranches: In the first tranche repayment increases with the price of the other security, and in the second tranche repayment decreases with the price of the other security.

Bull CD

A bull CD pays its holder a specified percentage of the increase in return on a specified marketindex while guaranteeing a minimum rate of return.

Bull market

Any market in which prices are in an upward trend.

Bull spread

A spread strategy in which an investor buys an out-of-the-money put option, financing it by selling an out-of-the money call option on the same underlying security.

Bulldog bond

Foreign bond issue made in London.

Bulldog market

The foreign market in the United Kingdom.

Bullet contract

A guaranteed investment contract purchased with a single (one-shot) premium. Related: Window contract.

Bullet loan

A bank term loan that calls for no amortization.

Bullet strategy

A fixed income strategy in which a portfolio is constructed so that the maturity's of its securities are highly concentrated at one point on the yield curve.

Bullion coins

Metal coins consisting of gold, silver, platinum, or palladium that are actively traded. Some examples include the American eagle and the Canadian maple leaf. Their price is directly connected to the underlying price of their metal.

Bullish

Words used to describe investor attitudes. Bullish refers to an optimistic outlook, while bearish means a pessimistic outlook.

Bump-up CD

A certificate of deposit granting the owner the right to increase its yield one time for the remaining term of the CD. The power is exercised by the owner in the event of an interest rate hike.

Bunching

Describes the act of traders combining round-lot orders for execution at the same time. Bunching can also be used to combine odd-lot orders to save the odd-lot differential for customers. Also used to refer to the pattern on the ticker tape when a series of trades for a security appear consecutively.

Bundesbank

The Bundesbank is the German central bank. The main functions of the Bundesbank are to regulate the money supply, support the general economic policy of the federal government, and issue banknotes. It sets the key discount rate, the Lombard rate, and minimum reserve requirements. Bank headquarters are in Frankfurt, Germany.

Bundesstelle für Aussenhandelsinformation

See Bundesministerium für Wirtschaft.

Bundesministerium für Wirtschaft

The BMWi (German: Ministry for Economic Affairs) gathers and distributes market information and supports semiprivate and private organizations, such as overseas chambers of commerce. Within the BMWi is the Federal Office for Foreign Trade (Bundesstelle fur Aussenhandelsinformation, BfAi), the government's primary agency for gathering and disseminating information. BfAi collects and distributes market information through a worldwide network.

Bundling, unbundling

Creation of securities either by combining primitive and derivative securities into one composite hybrid or by separating returns on an asset into classes.

Bureau of International des Expositions (BIE)

The Bureau of International Expositions, BIE, is an international organization established by the Paris Convention of 1928 to regulate the conduct and scheduling of international expositions in which foreign nations are officially invited to participate. The BIE divides international expositions into different categories and types and requires each member nation to observe specified minimum time intervals in scheduling each of these categories and types of operations. Under BIE rules, member nations may not ordinarily participate in an international exposition unless the exposition has been approved by the BIE. The United States became a member of the BIE in April 1968. Federal participation in a recognized international exposition requires specific authorization by the Congress, based on the President's finding that participation is in the national interest.

Bureau of Labor Statistics (BLS)

A reserch agency of the U.S. Department of Labor; it compiles statistics on hours of work, average hourly earnings, employment and unemployment, consumer prices and many other variables.

Burn rate

Used in venture capital financing to refer to the rate at which a startup company expends capital to finance overhead costs prior to the generation of positive cash flow.

Burnout

Depletion of a tax shelter's benefits. In the context of mortgage backed securities it refers to the percentage of the pool that has prepaid their mortgage.

Business combination

See: Merger

Business Combination laws

These laws impose a moratorium on certain kinds of transactions (e.g., asset sales, mergers) between a large shareholder and the firm for a period usually ranging between three and five years after the shareholder's stake passes a pre-specified (minority) threshold. These laws are in place in more than half the U.S. states.

Business Council for International Understanding (BCIU)

The BCIU is an independent, non-partisan, business association which was formed at the initiative of President Eisenhower. BCIU operates the U.S. Ambassadorial and Senior Diplomat Industry Program in which most U.S. Ambassadors come to BCIU after appointment and again in mid tour for briefings with top management of companies active or interested in the diplomat's country of assignment. While originally focused exclusively on U.S. diplomats, BCIU now also sponsors discussions with visiting Chiefs of Government, Ministers of Finance and Industry, Central Bank Governors, and other foreign officials.

Business cycle

Repetitive cycles of economic expansion and recession. The official peaks and troughs of the US cycle are determined by the National Bureau of Economic Research in Cambridge, MA.

Business day

A day in which financial markets are open for trading.

Business Executive Enforcement Team (BEET)

The Business Executive Enforcement Team, BEET, provides a channel for private sector executives to discuss export control enforcement matters with the Bureau of Export Administration.

Business Facilitation Office (BFO)

This is usually a booth with a reference desk with product catalogs manned by the Commercial Section or a qualified contractor to assist fair visitors or buyers searching for U.S. products or services at an international trade fair.

Business failure

A business that has terminated operations with a loss to creditors.

The business information office or center is a post or contract-staffed commercial reference facility usually at a scheduled international trade exhibition.

Business Information Service for the Newly Independent States (BISNIS)

BISNIS is a one-stop shop for U.S. firms interested in obtaining assistance on selling in the markets of the Newly Independent States of the former Soviet Union (Armenia, Azerbaijan, Belarus, Georgia, Kazakhstan, Kyrgyzstan, Moldova, Russia, Tajikistan, Turkmenistan, Ukraine, and Uzbekistan). BISNIS provides information on trade regulations and legislation, defense conversion opportunities, commercial opportunities, market data, sources of financing, government and industry contacts, and U.S. government programs supporting trade and investment in the region. BISNIS, established in June 1992, maintains a 24-hour automated flashfax system through which U.S. companies can receive information on doing business in the NIS via fax (202-482-3145).

Business risk

The risk that the cash flow of an issuer will be impaired because of adverse economic conditions, making it difficult for the issuer to meet its operating expenses.

Business segment reporting

Reporting the results of the separate divisions or subsidiaries of a business.

Busted convertible

Related: Fixed income equivalent. Mainly applies to convertible securities. Convertible bond selling essentially as a straight bond. Assuming the issuer is "money good," or will continue to meet credit obligations, such issues can be highly attractive since the price makes virtually no allowance for the bond's call on the common stock, although such issues usually carry high premiums.

Bust-up takeover

A leveraged buyout in which the buyer sells off the assets of the target_company to repay the debt that financed the takeover.

Butterfly

In the context of equities, a firm with two divisions may split into two companies and issue original shareholders two shares (one in each of the new companies) for every old share they have.

Butterfly shift

A nonparallel shift in the yield curve involving the height of the curve.

Butterfly spread

Applies to derivative products. Complex option strategy that involves selling two calls and buying two calls on the same or different markets, with several maturity dates. One of the options has a higher exercise price and the other has a lower exercise price than the other two options. The payoff diagram resembles the shape of a butterfly.

Buy

To purchase an asset; taking a long position.

Buy American Restrictions (BAR)

BARs were derived from the Buy American Act (BAA) of March 1933 and amended by the Buy American Act of 1988. Restrictions may take several forms, including: (a) straightforward prohibition of public sector bodies from purchasing goods from foreign suppliers, (b) establishing local content requirements of anything up to 100% of the value of the product, (c) extending preferential terms to domestic suppliers, and (d) setting up of manufacturing or assembly facilities in the United States. The BAA contains four exceptions which permit an executive agency to procure foreign materials when: (a) items are for use outside the United States, (b) domestic items are not available, (c) procurement of domestic items is determined to be inconsistent with the public interest, and (d) the cost of domestic items is determined to be unreasonable. The Trade Act of 1979 (which addressed implementation of the Tokyo Round) waives the BAA for certain designated countries which grant reciprocal access to U.S. suppliers.

Buy-and-hold strategy

A passive investment strategy with no active buying and selling of stocks from the time the portfolio is created until the end of the investment horizon.

Buy-and-write strategy

An options strategy that calls for the purchase of stocks and the writing of covered call options on them.

Buyback (or Compensation)

Buyback is an agreement whereby the primary supplier accepts as full or partial repayment products derived from the original exported product. Buyback arrangements support the financing of production facilities - e.g., the export of machinery and capital equipment, manufacturing processes, and technology.

Buy the book

An order, typically from a large institutional investor to a broker to purchase all the shares available at the market from the specialist and other brokers and dealers at the current offer price. The book refers to the record a specialist kept before the advent of computers.

Buydown

A lump sum payment made to the creditor by the borrower or by a third party to reduce the amount of some or all of the consumer's periodic payments to repay the indebtedness.

Buyer credit

Some export sales, especially sales of capital equipment, may sometimes require financing terms tailored to the buyer's cash flow and may involve payments over several years. Often the buyer obtains a loan from its own bank or arranges for other financing to enable it to pay cash to the exporter. U.S. exporters frequently benefit from such buyer credits when federal agencies such as the U.S. Export-Import Bank and Overseas Investment Corporation participate.

Buy hedge

See: Long hedge

Buy in

To cover, offset, or close out a short position. Related: Evening up, liquidation.

Buy limit order

A conditional trading order that indicates a security may be purchased only at the designated price or lower. Related: Sell limit order.

Buy minus order

In the context of general equities, rare market or limit order to buy a stated amount of a stock, provided that the price to be obtained is not higher than the last sale if the last sale is a minus or zero-minus tick, and is not higher than the last sale minus the minimum fractional change in the stock if the last sale is a plus or zero-plus tick. (If limit, then the buy cannot occur above the limit, regardless of tick.)

Buy on the bad news

Buying stock shortly after a price drop resulting from bad news from the company. Investors believe that the price has hit bottom and will trend upward. See: Bottom fisher.

Buy on close

Buying at the end of the trading session at a price within the closing range.

Buy on margin

Borrowing to buy additional shares, using the shares themselves as collateral.

Buy on opening

Buying at the beginning of a trading session at a price within the opening range.

Buy order

An order to a broker to purchase a specific quantity of a security.

Buy-side analyst

A financial analyst employed by a nonbrokerage firm, typically one of the larger money management firms that purchases securities on its own account.

Buy stop order

A buy order not to be executed until the market price rises to the stop price. Once the security has broken through that price, the order is then treated as a market order. Also known as a suspended market order.

"Buy them back"

Used for listed equity securities. "Cover my short position.

Buy write

See also Covered Call.

Buyback

The covering of a short position by purchasing a long contract, usually resulting from the short sale of a commodity. See: Short covering, stock buyback. Also used in the context of bonds. The purchase of corporate bonds by the issuing company at a discount in the open market. Also used in the context of corporate finance. When a firm elects to repurchase some of the shares trading in the market.

Buydowns

Mortgages in which monthly payments consist of principal and interest. During the early part of the loan, portions of these payments are provided by a third party to reduce the borrower's monthly payments.

Buyer's market

Market in which the supply exceeds the demand, creating lower prices. Antithesis of seller's_market.

Buyers/sellers on balance

Used for listed equity securities. Indicates that at a given time (usually before the opening of a stock/market or at expiration time), there are more buyers/sellers in the marketplace, usually with market orders. See: Imbalance of orders.

Buying climax

A rapid rise in the price of a stock resulting from heavy buying, which usually creates the market condition for a rapid fall in the price.

Buying the index

Purchasing the stocks in the S&P 500 in the same proportion as the index to achieve the same return.

Buying power

The amount of money available to buy securities, determined by adding the total cash held in brokerage accounts and the amount that could be spent if securities were margined to the limit.

Buyout

Purchase of a controlling interest (or percent of shares) of a company's stock. A leveraged buy out is effected with borrowed money.

BV

The two-character ISO 3166 country code for BOUVET ISLAND.

BW

The two-character ISO 3166 country code for BOTSWANA.

BWP

The ISO 4217 currency code for Botswanan Pula.

BY

The two-character ISO 3166 country code for BELARUS.

BYB

The ISO 4217 currency code for Belarus Rouble.

Bylaws

Rules and practices that govern management of an organization.

Bylaw Amendment Limitations

These provisions limit shareholders' ability to amend the governing documents of the corporation. This might take the form of a supermajority vote requirement for charter or bylaw amendments, total elimination of the ability of shareholders to amend the bylaws, or the ability of directors beyond the provisions of state law to amend the bylaws without shareholder approval.

Bypass trust

An irrevocable trust that is designed to pay trust income (and principal, if needed) to an individual's spouse for the duration of the spouse's lifetime. The bypass trust is not part of the beneficiary spouse's estate and is not subject to federal estate taxes upon his/her death.

BZ

The two-character ISO 3166 country code for BELIZE.

BZD

The ISO 4217 currency code for Belize Dollar.

C

C

Fifth letter of a Nasdaq stock descriptor specifying that issue is exempt from Nasdaq listing requirements for a temporary period.

CA

The two-character ISO 3166 country code for CANADA.

CABEI

See Central American Bank for Economic Integration.

Cabinet crowd

NYSE members who trade bonds with a low daily traded volume. See: Automated Bond System.

Cabinet security

A stock or bond listed on a major exchange with low daily traded volume.

Cable

Exchange rate between British pound sterling and the U.S. dollar.

Cabotage

A law which requires coastal and intercoastal traffic to be carried by vessels belonging to the country owning the coast.

CAC 40 index

A broad-based index of common stocks composed of 40 of the 100 largest companies listed on the forward segment of the official list of the Paris Bourse.

CAD

The ISO 4217 currency code for Canada Dollar.

CADS

See Cash Available for Debt Service.

Cage

A section of a brokerage firm used for receiving and disbursing funds.

CAGR

See: Compound Annual Growth Rate.

Cairns Group

The Cairns Group, established in August 1986 in Cairns, Australia, is an informal association of agricultural exporting countries. Members include: Argentina, Australia, Brazil, Canada, Chile, Colombia, Fiji, Hungary, Indonesia, Malaysia, New Zealand, Philippines, Thailand, and Uruguay. The Group seeks to reduce export subsidies and internal support measures and to bring about other reforms to international agricultural trade. The Cairns Group countries account for one third of world farm exports.

Caisse Centrale de Cooperation Economique

The CCCE, a specialized financial institution, is the lead agency in the French Ministry of Cooperation and

Development in providing funds for aid and cooperation. The Caisse provides support for development and technical assistance in developing countries, particularly in supporting economic and social development in Africa and in various countries on the Indian Ocean, the Caribbean and the South Pacific, and in overseas French departments and territories where it supports productive private and public investment. The Caisse was created in December 1941; headquarters are in Paris, France.

Calendar

List of new issues scheduled to come to market shortly.

Calendar effect

Describes the tendency of stocks to perform differently at different times. For example, a number of researchers have documented that historically, returns tend to be higher in January compared to other months (especially February). Other have documented returns patterns across days of the week and within the day. Some of these patterns are found in volume and volatility as well as returns.

Calendar spread

Applies to derivative products. A strategy in which there is a simultaneous purchase and sale of options of the same class at different strike prices, but with the same expiration date.

Calendar Straddle or Combination

See Calendar Spread.

Call

An option that gives the holder the right to buy the underlying futures contract.

Call date

A date before maturity, specified at issuance, when the issuer of a bond may retire part of the bond for a specified call price.

Call feature

Part of the indenture agreement between the bond issuer and buyer describing the schedule and price of redemption's prior to maturity.

Call loan

A loan repayable on demand. Sometimes used as a synonym for broker loan or broker overnight loan.

Call loan rate

See: Call money rate.

Call money rate

Also called the broker loan rate , the interest rate that banks charge brokers to finance margin loans to investors. The broker charges the investor the call money rate plus a servicecharge.

Call option

An option contract that gives its holder the right (but not the obligation) to purchase a specified number of shares of the underlying stock at the given strike price, on or before the expiration date of the contract.

Call an option

To exercise a call option.

Call premium

Premium in price above the par value of a bond or share of preferred stock that must be paid to holders to redeem the bond or share of preferred stock before its scheduled maturity date.

Call price

The price, specified at issuance, at which the issuer of a bond may retire part of the bond at a specified call date.

Call protection

A feature of some callable bonds that establishes an initial period when the bonds may not be called.

Call provision

An embedded option granting a bond issuer the right to buy back all or part of an issue prior to maturity.

Call risk

The combination of cash flow uncertainty and reinvestment risk introduced by a call provision.

Call swaption

A swaption in which the buyer has the right to enter into a swap as a fixed-rate payer. The writer therefore becomes the fixed-rate receiver/floating-rate payer.

Callability

Feature of a security that allows the issuer to redeem the security prior to maturity by calling it in, or forcing the holder to sell it back.

Callable

Applies mainly to convertible securities. Redeemable by the issuer before the scheduled maturity under specific conditions and at a stated price, which usually begins at a premium to par and declines annually. Bonds are usually called when interest rates fall so significantly that the issuer can save money by issuing new bonds at lower rates.

Called away

Convertible: Redeemed before maturity. Option: Call or put option exercised against the stockholder. Sale: Delivery required on a short sale.

Calvo Doctrine

The Calvo Doctrine (or principle) holds that jurisdiction in international investment disputes lies with the country in which the investment is located; thus, the investor has no recourse but to use the local courts. The principle, named after an Argentinean jurist, has been applied throughout Latin America and other areas of the world.

CAMPS (Cumulative Auction Market Preferred Stocks)

Stands for Cumulative Auction Market Preferred Stocks, Oppenheimer & Company's Dutch Auction preferred stock product.

Canadian agencies

Agency banks established by Canadian Banks in the US

Canadian Dealing Network (CDN)

The organized OTC market of Canada. Formerly known as the Canadian Over-the-Counter Automated Trading System (COATS), the CDN became a subsidiary of the Toronto Stock Exchange in 1991.

Canadian Commercial Corporation

By serving as the prime contractor in government-to-government sales transactions, the CCC facilitates exports of a wide range of goods and services from Canadian sources. In response to requests from foreign governments and international agencies for individual products or services, CCC identifies Canadian firms capable of meeting the customer's requirements, executes prime as well as back-to-back contracts, and follows through with contract management, inspection, acceptance, and payment.

Canadian Exchange Group (CEG)

The CEG is an association among the Toronto Stock Exchange, the Montreal Exchange, the Vancouver Stock Exchange, the Alberta Stock Exchange, and the Winnipeg Stock Exchange for the purpose of providing Canadian market data to customers outside Canada.

Canadian International Development Agency

CIDA (French: Agence Canadienne de Developement International) is Canada's official agency which has the task of supporting sustainable development in developing countries. The Agency was established in 1968; headquarters are in Hull, Quebec.

"Can get $xxx"

Refers to over-the-counter trading. "I have a buyer who will pay $xxx for the stock". Usually a standard mark-down (1/8) from $xxx is applied to this price in bidding the seller for its stock. Antithesis of cost me.

Cancel

To void an order to buy or sell from (1) the floor, or (2) the trader/salesperson's scope. In Autex, the indication still remains on record as having once been placed unless it is expunged.

Canceled Certificates

Before the issuance of a new certificate, the old certificate is presented to the Transfer Agent and is canceled.

"Cannot compete"

In the context of general equities, cannot accommodate customers at that price level (i.e., compete with other market makers), often because there is no natural opposite side of the trade.

"Cannot complete"

In the context of general equities, inability to finish an order on a principal or agency basis, given prevailing price instructions and/or market conditions.

Cap

An upper limit on the interest rate on a floating-rate note (FRN) or an adjustable-rate mortgage (ARM).

Capacity

Credit grantors' measurement of a person's ability to repay loans.

Capacity utilization rate

The percentage of the economy's total plant and equipment that is currently in production. Usually, a decrease in this percentage signals an economic slowdown, while an increase signals economic expansion.

Capital

Money invested in a firm.

Capital account

Net result of public and private international investment and lending activities.

Capital allocation decision

Allocation of invested funds between risk-free assets and the risky portfolio.

Capital appreciation

See: Capital growth.

Capital appreciation fund

See: Aggressive growth fund.

Capital asset

A long-term asset, such as land or a building, not purchased or sold in the normal course of business.

Capital asset pricing model (CAPM)

An economic theory that describes the relationship between risk and expected return, and serves as a model for the pricing of risky securities. The CAPM asserts that the only risk that is priced by rational investors is systematic risk, because that risk cannot be eliminated by diversification. The CAPM says that the expected return of a security or a portfolio is equal to the rate on a risk-free security plus a risk premium multiplied by the assets systematic risk. Theory was invented by William Sharpe (1964) and John Lintner (1965).

Capital budget

A firm's planned capital expenditures.

Capital budgeting

The process of choosing the firm's long-term capital assets.

Capital Builder Account (CBA)

A Merrill Lynch brokerage account that allows investors to access the loan value of his or her eligible securities to buy or sell securities. Excess cash in a CBA can be invested in a money market fund or an insured money market deposit account without losing access to the money.

Capital Development Initiative

The CDI, administered by the U.S. Agency for International Development, encourages infrastructure investment in countries in central and Eastern Europe. The CDI provides financial and technical services and assists U.S. businesses by providing up to 50 percent of estimated development work and feasibility study costs for proposed projects in energy, telecommunications, and the environment.

Capital expenditures

Amount used during a particular period to acquire or improve long-term assets such as property, plant, or equipment.

Capital flight

The transfer of capital abroad in response to fears of political risk.

Capital formation

Expansion of capital or capital goods through savings, which leads to economic growth.

Capital gain

When a stock is sold for a profit, the capital gain is the difference between the net sales price of the securities and their net cost, or original basis. If a stock is sold below cost, the difference is a capital loss.

Capital gains distribution

A distribution to the shareholders of a mutual fund out of profits from selling stocks or bonds, that is subject to capital gains taxes for the shareholders.

Capital gains tax

The tax levied on profits from the sale of capital assets. A long-term capital gain, which is achieved once an asset is held for at least 12 months, is taxed at a maximum rate of 20% (taxpayers in 28% tax bracket) and 10% (taxpayers in 15% tax bracket). Assets held for less than 12 months are taxed at regular income tax levels, and, since January 1, 2000, assets held for at least five years are taxed at 18% and 8%.

Capital gains yield

The price change portion of a stock's return.

Capital goods

Goods used by firms to produce other goods, e.g., office buildings, machinery, equipment.

Capital growth

The increase in an asset's market price. Also called capital appreciation.

Capital infusion

Often referss to the cross-subsidization of divisions within a firm. When one division is not doing well, it might benefit from an infusion of new funds from the more successful divisions. In the context of venture capital, it can also refer to funds received from a venture capitalist to either get the firm started or to save it from failing due to lack of cash.

Capital-intensive

Used to describe industries that require large investments in capital assets to produce their goods, such as the automobile industry. These firms require large profit margins and/or low costs of borrowing to survive.

Capital International Indexes

Market indexes maintained by Morgan Stanley that track major stock markets worldwide.

Capital investment

See: Capital expenditure.

Capital lease

A lease obligation that has to be capitalized on the balance sheet.

Capital loss

The difference between the net cost of a security and the net sales price, if the security is sold at a loss.

Capital market

The market for trading long-term debt instruments (those that mature in more than one year).

Capital market efficiency

The degree to which the present asset price accurately reflects current information in the market place. See: Efficient market hypothesis.

Capital market imperfections view

The view that issuing debt is generally valuable, but that the firm's optimal choice of capital structure involves various other views of capital structure (net corporate/personal tax, agency cost, bankruptcy cost, and pecking order), that result from considerations of asymmetric information, asymmetric taxes, and transaction costs.

Capital market line (CML)

The line defined by every combination of the risk-free asset and the market portfolio. The line represents the risk premium you earn for taking on extra risk. Defined by the capital asset pricing model.

Capital rationing

Placing limits on the amount of new investment undertaken by a firm, either by using a higher cost of capital, or by setting a maximum on the entire capital budget or parts of it.

Capital requirements

Financing required for the operation of a business, composed of long-term and working capital plus fixed assets.

Capital shares

One of two types of shares in a dual-purpose investment company, which entitle the holder to the appreciation or depreciation in the value of a portfolio, as well as the gains from trading in the portfolio. Antithesis of income shares.

Capital stock

Stock authorized by a firm's charter and having par value, stated value, or no par value. The number and the value of issued shares are usually shown, together with the number of shares authorized, in the capital accounts section of the balance sheet. See: Common stock.

Capital structure

The makeup of the liabilities and stockholders' equity side of the balance sheet, especially the ratio of debt to equity and the mixture of short and long maturities.

Capital surplus

Amounts of directly contributed equity capital in excess of the par value.

Capital turnover

Calculated by dividing annual sales by average stockholder equity (net worth). The ratio indicates how much a company could grow its current capital investment level. Low capital turnover generally corresponds to high profit margins.

Capitalization

The debt and/or equity mix that funds a firm's assets.

Capitalization method

A method of constructing a replicating portfolio in which the manager purchases a number of the most highly capitalized names in the stock index in proportion to their capitalization.

Capitalization rate

The rate of interest used to calculate the present value of a number of future payments.

Capitalization ratios

Also called financial leverage ratios, these ratios compare debt to total capitalization and thus reflect the extent to which a corporation is trading on its equity. Capitalization ratios can be interpreted only in the context of the stability of industry and company earnings and cash flow.

Capitalization table

A table showing the capitalization of a firm, which typically includes the amount of capital obtained from each source - long-term debt and common equity - and the respective capitalization ratios.

Capitalization-Weighted Index

A stock index which is computed by adding the capitalization (float times price) of each individual stock in the index, and then dividing by the divisor. The stocks with the largest market values have the heaviest weighting in the index. See also Float, Divisor.

Capitalized

Recorded in asset accounts and then depreciated or amortized, as is appropriate for expenditures for items with useful lives longer than one year.

Capitalized interest

Interest that is not immediately expensed, but rather is considered as an asset and is then amortized through the income statement over time.

CAPM

See: Capital asset pricing model.

Capped-Style Option

A capped option is an option with an established profit cap or cap price. The cap price is equal to the option's strike price plus a cap interval for a call option or the strike price minus a cap interval for a put option. A capped option is automatically exercised when the underlying security closes at or above (for a call) or at or below (for a put) the Option's cap price.

CAPS

See: Convertible adjustable preferred stock.

Captive finance company

A company, usually a subsidiary that is wholly owned, whose main function is financing consumer purchases from the parent company.

Caput

An exotic option. It represents a call option on a put option. That is, you purchase the option to buy a put option at a particular price on or before the expiriation date.

Car

A loose quantity term sometimes used to describe the amount of a commodity underlying one commodity contract; e.g., "a car of bellies." Derived from the fact that quantities of the product specified in a contract once corresponded closely to the capacity of a railroad car.

Caracas Stock Exchange

Originally established in 1947 and merged with a competitor in 1974 to become the only securities exchange of Venezuela.

CARDs

See: Certificates of Amortized Revolving Debt.

Cargo

Goods being transported.

Cargo Selectivity System

The Cargo Selectivity System, a part of Customs' Automated Commercial System, specifies the type of examination (intensive or general) to be conducted for imported merchandise. The type of examination is based on database selectivity criteria such as assessments of risk by filer, consignee, tariff number, country of origin, and manufacturer/shipper. A first time consignee is always selected for an intensive examination. An alert is also generated in cargo selectivity the first time a consignee files an entry in a port with a particular tariff number, country of origin, or manufacturer/shipper.

Caribbean Basin Economic Recovery Act

The CBERA affords nonreciprocal tariff preferences to developing countries in the Caribbean Basin area to aid their economic development and to diversity and expand their production and exports. The CBERA applies to merchandise entered, or withdrawn from warehouse for consumption, on or after January 1, 1984. This tariff preference program has no expiration date.

Caribbean Basin Initiative

The CBI is an inter-American program to increase economic aid and trade preferences for 28 states of the Caribbean region. The Caribbean Basin Economic Recovery Act of 1983 provided for 12 years of duty-free treatment of most goods produced in the Caribbean region. The Initiative was extended permanently (CBI II), by the Customs and Trade Act of August 1990.

The 23 countries which are currently eligible for CBI benefits include Antigua and Barbuda, the Bahamas, Barbados, Belize, the British Virgin Islands, Costa Rica, Dominica, the Dominican Republic, El Salvador, Grenada, Guatemala, Guyana, Honduras, Jamaica, Montserrat, the Netherlands Antilles, Nicaragua, Panama, St. Christopher-Nevis, St. Lucia, St. Vincent and the Grenadines, and Trinidad and Tobago. The following countries may be eligible for CBI benefits but have not formally requested designation: Anguilla, Cayman Islands, Suriname, and the Turks and Caicos Islands.

Caribbean/Central America Business Advisory Service

The BAS helps entrepreneurs in the Caribbean and in Central America to develop project ideas into investment proposals and to obtain long-term finance for them. The Service does not lend or invest, but does provide advice and assistance in project structuring, identification of technical and marketing partners, project appraisal, and identification of financing resources. BAS operates under the auspices of the United Nations Development Program and is managed by the World Bank's International Finance Corporation. BAS was established in 1981 as the Caribbean Business Advisory Service (CBAS). The BAS 1989 expansion to Central America extended its operations to all CBI beneficiary countries. See also: Caribbean Basin Initiative.

Caribbean Common Market

CARICOM includes 13 English-speaking Caribbean nations: Antigua and Barbuda, the Bahamas, Barbados, Belize, Dominica, Grenada, Guyana, Jamaica, Montserrat, St. Kitts-Nevis, St. Lucia, St. Vincent/Grenadines, and Trinidad and Tobago). CARICOM was established in 1973; headquarters are in Georgetown, Guyana.

Caribbean Development Bank

The CDB promotes economic development and cooperation by providing long-term financing for productive projects in CARICOM member countries and U.K.-dependent territories in the Caribbean. Members include: Anguilla, Antigua and Barbuda, the Bahamas, Barbados, Belize, British Virgin Islands, Canada, Cayman Islands, Dominica, France, Grenada, Guyana, Jamaica, Mexico, Montserrat, Saint Kitts and Nevis, Saint Lucia, Saint Vincent and the Grenadines, Trinidad and Tobago, Turks and Caicos Islands, the United Kingdom, and Venezuela. The Bank was established in 1969; headquarters are in St. Michael, Barbados, West Indies. Beginning in 1977, the Inter-American Development Bank (IADB) may make loans through the CDB to all CDB members, regardless of whether those countries are members of the IADB. See: Inter-American Development Bank.

CARICOM

See Caribbean Common Market.

Carnets

Customs documents permitting the holder to carry or send sample merchandise temporarily into certain foreign countries without paying duties or posting bonds. Foreign customs regulations vary widely; in some countries, duties and extensive customs procedures on sample products may be avoided by obtaining an ATA Carnet. The ATA Carnet is a standardized international customs document used to obtain duty-free temporary admission of certain goods into the countries that are signatories to the ATA Convention. Under the ATA Convention, commercial and professional travelers may take commercial samples; tools of the trade; advertising material; and cinematographic, audiovisual, medical, scientific, or other professional equipment into member countries temporarily without paying customs duties and taxes or posting a bond at the border of each country visited. The carnets are generally valid for 12 months. Telephone: 1-800-CARNETS.

Carriage and Insurance Paid To (CIP)

Seller is responsible for the payment of freight to carry goods to a named overseas destination. The seller is also responsible for providing cargo insurance at minimum coverage against the buyer's risk of loss or damage to the goods during transport. The risk of loss or damage is transferred from the seller to the buyer once the goods are delivered into the carrier's custody. This term may be used for any mode of transport.

Carriage Paid To (CPT)

Seller is responsible for the payment of freight to carry goods to a named overseas destination. The risk of loss or damage is transferred from the seller to the buyer when the goods have been delivered into the carrier's custody. This term may be used for any mode of transport.

Carrot equity

British slang for an equity investment with the added benefit of an opportunity to purchase more equity if the company reaches certain financial goals.

Carry

Related: Net financing cost.

Carryforwards

Tax losses allowed to be applied to offset future income in some specified number of future years.

Carrying charge

The fee a broker charges for carrying securities on credit, such as on a margin account.

Carrying costs

Costs that increase with increases in the level of investment in current assets.

Carrying value

Book value.

CARs

See: Certificates of Automobile Receivables.

Cartagena Agreement

See Andean Pact.

Cartagena Group

See Group of Eleven.

Cartel

A group of businesses or nations that act together as a single producer to obtain market control and to influence prices in their favor by limiting production of a product. The United States has laws prohibiting cartels.

Cash

The value of assets that can be converted into cash immediately, as reported by a company. Usually includes bank accounts and marketable securities, such as government bonds and banker's acceptances. Cash equivalents on balance sheets include securities that mature within 90 days (e.g., notes).

Cash Against Documents

A term denoting that payment is made when the bill of lading is presented.

Cash account

A brokerage account that settles transactions on a cash-rather than credit-basis.

Cash Available for Debt Service

Ratio of cash assets to debt service (interest plus nearby principal). Used in evaluating the risk of a project or firm. The higher the ratio the less likely the firm or project will fail to meet its debt obligations.

Cash asset ratio

Cash and marketable securities divided by current liabilities. See: Liquidity ratios.

Cashed-Based

Refering to an option or future that is settled in cash when exercised or assigned. No physical entity, either stock or commodity, is recevied or delivered.

Cash basis

Refers to the accounting method that recognizes revenues and expenses when cash is actually received or paid out.

Cash and equivalents

The value of assets that can be converted into cash immediately, as reported by a company. Usually includes bank accounts and marketable securities, such as government bonds and Banker's Acceptances. Cash equivalents on balance sheets include securities (e.g., notes) that mature within 90 days.

Cash budget

A forecasted summary of a firm's expected cash inflows and cash outflows as well as its expected cash and loan balances.

Cash & carry

Applies to derivative products. Combination of a long position in a stock/index/commodity and short position in the underlying futures, which entails a cost of carry on the long position.

Cash commodity

The actual physical commodity, as distinguished from a futures contract.

Cash conversion cycle

The length of time between a firm's purchase of inventory and the receipt of cash from accounts receivable.

Cash cow

A company that pays out most of its earnings per share to stockholders as dividends. Or, a company or division of a company that generates a steady and significant amount of free cash flow.

Cash cycle

In general, the time between cash disbursement and cash collection. In net working capital management, it can be thought of as the operating cycle less the accounts payable payment period.

Cash deficiency agreement

An agreement to invest cash in a project to the extent required to cover any cash deficiency the project may experience.

Cash delivery

The provision of some futures contracts that requires not delivery of underlying assets but settlement according to the cash value of the asset.

Cash discount

An incentive offered to purchasers of a firm's product for payment within a specified time period, such as ten days.

Cash dividend

A dividend paid in cash to a company's shareholders. The amount is normally based on profitability and is taxable as income. A cash distribution may include capital gains and return of capital in addition to the dividend.

Cash earnings

A firm's cash revenues less cash expenses, which excludes the costs of depreciation.

Cash-equivalent items

Examples include Treasury bills and Banker's Acceptances.

Cash flow

In investments, cash flow represents earnings before depreciation, amortization, and non-cash charges. Sometimes called cash earnings. Cash flow from operations (called funds from operations by real estate and other investment trusts) is important because it indicates the ability to pay dividends.

Cash flow after interest and taxes

Net income plus depreciation.

Cash flow break-even point

The point below which the firm will need either to obtain additional financing or to liquidate some of its assets to meet its fixed costs.

Cash flow per common share

Cash flow from operations minus preferred stock dividends, divided by the number of common shares outstanding.

Cash flow coverage ratio

The number of times that financial obligations (for interest, principal payments, preferred stock dividends, and rental payments) are covered by earnings before interest, taxes, rental payments, and depreciation.

Cash flow matching

Also called dedicating a portfolio, this is an alternative to multiperiod immunization that calls for the manager to match the maturity of each element in the liability stream, working backward from the last liability to assure all required cash flows.

Cash flow from operations

A firm's net cash inflow resulting directly from its regular operations (disregarding extraordinary items such as the sale of fixed assets or transaction costs associated with issuing securities), calculated as the sum of net income plus noncash expenses that are deducted in calculating net income.

Cash flow time line

Line depicting the operating activities and cash flows for a firm over a particular period.

Cash in Advance

A payment term meaning the buyer pays the seller before shipment is effected.

Cash In Lieu (CIL)

In a typical exchange offer, "old" shares of the target company are exchanged for "new shares".

Cash investments

Short-term debt instruments—such as commercial paper, banker's acceptances, and Treasury bills—that mature in less than one year. Also known as money market instruments or cash reserves.

Cash management

Refers to the efficient management of cash in a business in order to put the cash to work more quickly and to keep the cash in applications that produce income, such as the use of lock boxes for payments.

Cash management bill

Very short-maturity bills that the Treasury occasionally sells because its cash balances are down and it needs money for a few days.

Cash markets

Also called spot markets, these are markets that involve the immediate delivery of a security or instrument. Related: Derivative markets.

Cash offer

Often used in risk arbitrage. Proposal, either hostile or friendly, to acquire a target company through the payment of cash for the stock of the target. Compare to exchange offer.

Cash-on-cash return

A method used to find the return on investments when there is no active secondary market. The yield is determined by dividing the annual cash income by the total investment. See: Current yield or yield to maturity.

Cash on delivery (COD)

In the context of securities, this refers to the practice of institutional investors paying the full purchase price for securities in cash.

Cash-out Laws

These laws enable shareholders to sell their stakes to a "controllin" shareholder at a price based on the highest price of recently acquired shares. This works something like Fair-Price provisions extended to nontakeover situations. A few states have these laws.

Cash plus convertible

Convertible bond that requires cash payment upon conversion.

Cash position

The percentage of a mutual fund's assets invested in short-term reserves, such as US Treasury bills or other money market instruments.

Cash price

Applies to derivative products. See: Spot price.

Cash ratio

The proportion of a firm's assets held as cash.

Cash reserves

See: Cash investments.

Cash sale/settlement

Transaction in which a contract is settled on the same day as the trade date, or the next day if the trade occurs after 2:30 p.m. EST and the parties agree to this procedure. Often occurs because a party is strapped for cash and cannot wait until the regular five-business day settlement. See: Settlement date.

Cash Settlement

The process by which the terms of an option contract are fulifilled through the payment or receipt in dollars of the amount by which the option is in-the-money as opposed to delivering or receiving the underlying stock.

Cash settlement contracts

Futures contracts such as stock index futures that settle for cash and do not involve delivery of the underlying.

Cash-surrender value

The amount an insurance company will pay if the policyholder tenders or cashes in a whole life insurance policy.

Cash transaction

A transaction in which exchange is immediate in the form of cash, unlike a forward contract (which calls for future delivery of an asset at an agreed-upon price).

Cashbook

An accounting book that is composed of cash receipts plus disbursements. This balance is posted to the cash account in the ledger.

Cashier's check

A check drawn directly on a customer's account, making the bank the primary obligor, and assuring firms that the amount will be paid.

Cashout

Occurs when a firm runs out of cash and cannot readily sell marketable securities.

Cash With Order

CWO is a means of payment in which the buyer pays cash when ordering; the order is binding on both seller and buyer.

Casualty-insurance

Insurance protecting a firm or homeowner against loss of property, damage, and other liabilities.

Casualty loss

A financial loss caused by damage, destruction, or loss of property as a result of an unexpected or unusual event.

Catalog Exhibitions

These promotions are low-cost exhibits of U.S. firms' catalogs and videos which offer small, less-experienced companies an opportunity to test overseas markets for their products without travel. The International Trade Administration promotes exhibitions, provides staff fluent in the local language to answer questions, and forwards all trade leads to participating firms.

Catastrophe call

Early redemption of a municipal revenue bond because a catastrophe has destroyed the project that provided the revenue source backing the bond.

Category Groups

Groupings of controlled products. See also: Export Control Classification Number.

CATS

See: Certificate of Accrual on Treasury Securities (CATS)

Cats and dogs

Speculative stocks with short histories of sales, earnings, and dividend payments.

Caveat emptor, caveat subscriptor

Latin expressions for "buyer beware" and "seller beware," which warn of overly risky, inadequately protected markets.

CAX

The ISO 4217 currency code for Canadian Cent.

CBD

See: Cash In Advance.

CBERA

See Caribbean Basin Economic Recovery Act.

CBO

See: Collateralized Bond Obligation.

CBI

See Caribbean Basin Initiative.

CBOE

See: Chicago Board Options Exchange.

CC

The two-character ISO 3166 country code for COCOS (KEELING) ISLANDS.

CCC

See Canadian Commercial Corporation.

CCCE

See Caisse Centrale de Cooperation Economique.

CD

(1) See: Certificate of deposit. (2) The two-character ISO 3166 country code for CONGO, THE DEMOCRATIC REPUBLIC OF.

CDB

See Caribbean Development Bank.

CDN

See: Canadian Dealing Network.

CDT

See Center for Defense Trade.

Cease-and-desist order

An order issued after notice and opportunity for hearing, requiring a depository instition, a holding company or a depository institution official to terminate unlawful, unsafe or unsound banking practices. Cease-and-desist orders are issued by the appropriate federal regulatory agencies under the Financial Institutions Supervisory Act and can be enforced directly by the courts.

CEC

See: Commodities Exchange Center.

Cede & Co.

Nominee name for The Depository Trust Company, a large clearing house that holds shares in its name for banks, brokers and institutions in order to expedite the sale and transfer of stock.

CEDEL

A centralized clearing system for Eurobonds.

CEFTA

See Central Europe Free Trade Association.

CEG

See: Canadian Exchange Group.

Ceiling

The highest price, interest rate, or other numerical factor allowable in a financial transaction.

Census Interface System

The Census Interface System, a part of Customs' Automated Commercial System, includes edits and validations provided by the Bureau of the Census to allow for the accurate and timely collection and submission of entry summary data. Census Interface is accomplished through Automated Broker Interface entry summary transmissions.

Center for Defense Trade

In 1990, the Center for Defense Trade, CDT, was created within the Bureau of Politico-Military Affairs (PM) at the Department of State. CDT was established with the purpose of improving the Department of State's export licensing services. CDT also has responsibility for clarifying all defense trade policy guidelines. The Center includes two offices:

— The Office of Defense Trade Controls (DTC) which administers controls on permanent exports and temporary imports of defense articles and technology covered by the U.S. Munitions List (USML) and performs USML export license review and compliance functions.

— The Office of Defense Trade Policy (DTP) which seeks to support the efforts of the U.S. defense industry to sell products overseas. DTP provides policy guidance to licensing officers, in support of their efforts to implement the International Traffic in Arms Regulations (ITAR) and provides advice on technology transfer and strategic trade issues.

Center for International Research

CIR analyzes and forecasts world demographic trends and economic developments in selected countries, based on current statistics obtained through international agreements. The center, which is a component of the Commerce Department's Bureau of the Census, conducts research with funds from government and private business sponsors. See: International Data Base.

Center for Trade and Investment Services

CTIS, established in September 1992, promotes increased participation of U.S. businesses in generating economic development in lesser developed countries which receive assistance from the Agency for International Development.

Central African Customs and Economic Union

The Central African Customs and Economic Union (French: Union Douaniere et Economique de l'Afrique Centrale, UDEAC) created in 1966 (revised 1974) to promote establishment of a Central African Common Market with a common external tariff. Members include: the Cameroon, Central African Republic, Chad, Congo, Equatorial Guinea, and Gabon. The Union's headquarters are in Bangui, Central African Republic.

Central African States Development Bank

The Central Africa States Development Bank (French: Banque de Developpement des stats de l'Afrique Centrale, BDEAC) was created in December 1975 (began operations in January 1977) to provide loans for economic development and to support integration projects. Members include: the Cameroon, Central African Republic, Chad, Congo, Equatorial Guinea, and Gabon. Bank headquarters are in Brazzaville, Congo.

Central American Bank for Economic Integration

CABEI (Spanish: Banco Centroamericano de Integraci¢n Econ¢mico, BCIE) was established in 1960 (began operations in September 1961) to promote economic integration and development. The Bank is an institution of the Central American Common Market.

Bank members include: Costa Rica, El Salvador, Guatemala, Honduras, and Nicaragua. CABEI is associated with the Central American Common Market; bank headquarters are in Tegucigalpa, Honduras. See: Central American Common Market.

Central American Common Market

A first effort to establish a Central American Common Market, CACM was attempted in 1960 under the auspieces of the Organization of Central American States (OCAS). A restructuring was started in 1973. Members include Honduras, Guatemala, El Salvador, Nicaragua and Costa Rica. The common market will cover all products traded within the region by the end of 1992. A second step toward regional integration will be the establishment of a common external tariff. CACM is associated with the Central American Bank for Economic Integration; headquarters are in Guatemala City, Guatemala. See: Central American Bank for Economic Integration.

Central bank

A country's main bank whose responsibilities include the issue of currency, the administration of monetary policy, open market operations, and engaging in transactions designed to facilitate healthy business interactions. See: Federal Reserve System.

Central bank intervention

The buying or selling of currency, foreign or domestic, by central banks in order to influence market conditions or exchange rate movements.

Central Europe Free Trade Association

CEFTA is a trade agreement among the "Visegrad" countries — Poland, the Czech Republic, Slovakia, and Hungary — that is somewhat parallel to the European Free Trade Association.

Centre Europeen de Recherche Nucleaire

CERN (English: European Center for Nuclear Reseach) is a huge lab used by international collaborators to do frontier work in nuclear and particle physics. The Center, created after World War II and open to physicists from all countries, is funded by countries according to their abilities. The Center is located outside Genvea, partly in Switzerland and partly in France.

Central Limit Theorem

The Law of Large Numbers states that as a sample of independent, identically distributed random numbers approaches infinity, its probability density function approaches the normal distribution. See: Normal Distribution.

Centralized cash flow management

Provision of consolidated cash management decisions to all MNC units from one location, usually at the parent's headquarters.

Cents per share

The amount of a mutual fund's dividend or capital gains distributions that a shareholder will receive for each share owned.

CERN

See Centre Europeen de Recherche Nucleaire.

Certainty equivalent

An amount that would be accepted today (risk free) in lieu of a chance to receive a possibly higher, but uncertain, amount.

Certainty Equivalent Return

The certain (zero risk) return an investor would trade for a given (larger) return with an associated risk. For example, a particular investor might trade an uncertain expected 4% active return with 6% risk, for a certain active return of 1.5%.

Certificate

A formal document used to record a fact and used as proof of the fact, such as stock certificates, that evidence ownership of stock in a corporation.

Certificate of Accrual on Treasury Securities (CATS)

Refers to a zero-coupon US Treasury issue that is sold at a deep discount from the face value and pays no coupon interest during its lifetime, but returns the full face value at maturity.

Certificate of Delivery

See Delivery Verification Certificate.

Certificate of deposit (CD)

Also called a time deposit this is a certificate issued by a bank or thrift that indicates a specified sum of money has been deposited. A CD has a maturity date and a specified interest rate, and can be issued in any denomination. The duration can be up to five years.

Certificate of Inspection

A document certifying that merchandise (such as perishable goods) was in good condition immediately prior to shipment. Pre-shipment inspection is a requirement for importation of goods into many developing countries.

Certificate of Manufacture

A document (often notarized) in which a producer of goods certifies that the manufacturing has been completed and the goods are now at the disposal of the buyer.

Certificate of Origin

Certain nations require a signed statement as to the origin of the export item. Such certificates are usually obtained through a semiofficial organization such as a local chamber of commerce. A certificate may be required even though the commercial invoice contains the information.

Certificates of Amortized Revolving Debt (CARD)

Pass-through securities backed by credit card receivables.

Certificates of Automobile Receivables (CAR)

Pass-through securities backed by automobile loan receivables.

Certificateless municipals

Municipal bonds with one certificate which is valid for the entire issue, and having no individual certificates, easing transactions. See: Book-entry securities.

Certified check

A bank guaranteed check for which funds are immediately withdrawn, and for which the bank is legally liable.

Certified Financial Planner (CFP)

A person who has passed examinations accredited by the Certified Financial Planner Board of Standards, showing that the person is able to manage a client's banking, estate, insurance, investment, and tax affairs.

Certified financial statements

Financial statements that include an accountant's opinion.

Certified Public Accountant (CPA)

An accountant who has met certain standards, including experience, age, and licensing, and passed exams in a particular state.

Certified Trade Fair Program

The Department of Commerce Certified Trade Fair Program is designed to encourage private organizations to recruit new-to-market and new-to-export U.S. firms to exhibit in trade fairs overseas. To receive certification, the organization must demonstrate:

(1) the fair is a leading international trade event for an industry and

(2) the fair organizer is capable of recruiting U.S. exhibitors and assisting them with freight forwarding, customs clearance, exhibit design and setup, public relations, and overall show promotion. The show organizer must agree to assist new-to-export exhibitors as well as small businesses interested in exporting.

In addition to the services the organizer provides, the Department of Commerce will:

- assign a Washington coordinator;
- operate a business information office, which provides meeting space, translators, hospitality, and assistance from U.S. exhibitors and foreign customers;
- help contact buyers, agents, distributors, and other business leads and provide marketing assistance;
- provide a press release on certification.

Certified Trade Missions

Certified trade missions (formerly State/Industry Organized, Government Approved trade missions) are planned and organized by state development agencies, trade associations, chambers of commerce, and other export-oriented groups. To qualify for U.S. government sponsorship, organizers of this type of trade mission must agree to follow International Trade Administration criteria in planning and recruiting the mission. ITA offers guidance and assistance from planning through completion of the mission and coordinates the support of all relevant offices and the assistance of overseas commercial officers in each foreign city on the itinerary. The missions are normally led by a representative of the sponsoring organization. Organizers of certified trade missions recruit for the event and cover the expenses of the event incurred by ITA's overseas post. Certified trade missions may use the seminar format, the exhibit format, the traditional trade mission format, or a combination, such as a seminar/ mission or exhibit/mission.

CF

The two-character ISO 3166 country code for CENTRAL AFRICAN REPUBLIC.

CFAT

Cash flow after taxes.

CFAT

See: Cash flow after taxes.

CFC

See: Controlled foreign corporation.

CFR

See: Cost and Freight.

CFTC

See: Commodity Futures Trading Commission.

CG

The two-character ISO 3166 country code for CONG.

CH

The two-character ISO 3166 country code for SWITZERLAND.

Chaebol

Chaebol are Korean conglomerates which are characterized by strong family control, authoritarian management, and centralized decision making. Chaebol dominate the Korean economy, growing out of the takeover of the Japanese monopoly of the Korean economy following World War II. Korean government tax breaks and financial incentives emphasizing industrial reconstruction and exports provided continuing support to the growth of Chaebols during the 1970s and 1980s. In 1988, the output of the 30 largest chaebol represented almost 95% of Korea's gross national product.

Chair of the board

Highest-ranking member of a Board of Directors, who presides over its meetings and who is often the most powerful officer of a corporation.

Chaos

A deterministic non-linear dynamic system that can produce random looking results. A chaotic system must have a fractal dimension, and exhibit sensitive dependence on initial conditions. See: Fractal Dimension, Lyapunov Exponent, Strange Attractor.

CHAP

See: Clearing House Automated Payments System.

Chapter 7 Proceedings

Provisions of the Bankruptcy Reform Act under which the debtor firm's assets are liquidated by a court because reorganization would fail to establish a profitable business.

Chapter 11 Proceedings

Provisions of the Bankruptcy Reform Act under which the debtor firm is reorganized by a court because the estimated value of the reorganized firm exceeds the expected proceeds from its liquidation.

Changes in financial position

Sources of funds provided from operations that alter a company's cash flow position: depreciation, deferred taxes, other sources, and capital expenditures.

Characteristic line

The market model applied to a single security; a regression of security returns on the benchmark return. The slope of the regression line is a security's beta.

Characteristic portfolio

A portfolio which efficiently represents a particular asset characteristic. For a given characteristic, it is the minimum risk portfolio, with portfolio characteristic equal to 1. For example, the characteristic portfolio of asset betas is the benchmark. It is the minimum risk beta = 1 portfolio.

Charge off

See: Bad debt.

Charitable remainder trust

An irrevocable trust that pays income to a designated person or persons until the grantor's death, when the income is passed on to a designated charity. A charitable lead trust by contrast allows the charity to receive income during the grantor's life, and the remaining income to pass to designated family members upon the grantor's death.

Charter

See: Articles of incorporation.

Charter Amendment Limitations

These provisions limit shareholders' ability to amend the governing documents of the corporation. This might take the form of a supermajority vote requirement for charter or bylaw amendments, total elimination of the ability of shareholders to amend the bylaws, or the ability of directors beyond the provisions of state law to amend the bylaws without shareholder approval.

Chartered Financial Analyst (CFA)

An experienced financial analyst who has passed examinations in economics, financial accounting, portfolio management, security analysis, and standards of conduct given by the institute of Chartered Financial Analysts.

Chartists

A technical analyst who charts the patterns of stocks, bonds, and commodities to find trends in patterns of trading used to advise clients. Related: Technical analysts.

Chasing the market

Purchasing a security at a higher price than expected because prices are rapidly climbing, or selling a security at a lower level when prices are quickly falling.

Chastity bonds

Bonds redeemable at par value in the case of a takeover.

Chatter

See: Whipsawed.

Chattel Mortgage

A loan agreement that grants to the lender a lien on property other than real estate. Chattel is personal or movable property.

Cheapest to deliver issue

The acceptable Treasury security with the highest implied repo rate; the rate that a seller of a futures contract can earn by buying an issue and then delivering it at the settlement date.

Check

A bill of exchange representing a draft on a bank from deposited funds that pays a certain sum of money to a certain person or party.

Check clearing

The movement of a check from the depository institution at which it was deposited back to the institution on which it was written; the movement of funds in the opposite direction and the corresponding credit and debit to the involved accounts. The Federal Reserve operates a nationwide check-clearing system.

Checking the market

Searching for bid and offer prices from market makers to find the best deal.

Checkwriting

Free checkwriting privileges offered with non-retirement accounts for select mutual funds.

Chemical/Biological Weapons

The Department of Commerce maintains foreign policy export controls on certain chemical precursors and equipment and biological agents and equipment useful in chemical warfare. Through the Australia Group,

AG, the United States cooperates with other nations in controlling chemical and biological weapons proliferation. The AG developed a list of 54 precursors useful for chemical weapons development, along with control on certain biological organisms and on equipment useful in producing CBW agents. The AG also provides the forum in which the member countries share information concerning the activities of non-member countries where the proliferation of these weapons is of concern, including entities that are seeking chemical precursors and related items.

Chemical Weapons Convention

The CWC prohibits the development, production, stockpiling, and use of chemical weapons. The Convention permits monitoring, collection and review of data and on-site inspections that involve questions of protection of proprietary rights and confidentiality. The Convention has been signed by over 160 nations; entry into force is expected in January 1995.

CHESS

See: Clearing House Electronic Subregister System.

CHF

The ISO 4217 currency code for Swiss Franc.

Chicago Board Options Exchange (CBOE)

A securities exchange created in the early 1970s for the public trading of standardized option contracts. Primary place stock options, foreign currency options, and index options (S&P 100, 500, and OTC 250 index)

Chicago Board of Trade (CBOT)

The second largest futures exchange in the US, and was a pioneer in the development of financial futures and options.

Chicago Mercantile Exchange (CME)

Chicago Mercantile Exchange (CME) is the largest futures exchange in the United States and the second largest exchange in the world for the trading of futures and options on futures. Founded in 1898 as a not-for-profit corporation, in November 2000 CME became the first U.S. financial exchange to demutualize and become a shareholder-owned corporation. Its futures and options on futures trade on CME's trading floors, on its GLOBEX electronic trading platform and through privately negotiated transactions. CME has four major product areas based on interest rates (including Eurodollar futures, the world's most actively traded futures contract), stock indexes (such as the (S&P 500 and Nasdaq-100 futures), foreign exchange and commodities.

Chicago Stock Exchange (CHX)

A major exchange trading only stocks, with 90% of trades taking place on an automated execution system, called MAX.

Chief Executive Officer (CEO)

A title held often by the Chairperson of the Board, or the president. The person principally responsible for the activities of a company.

Chief Financial Officer (CFO)

The officer of a firm is responsible for handling the financial affairs of a company.

Chief Operating Officer (COO)

The officer of a firm responsible for day-to-day management, usually the president or an executive vice-president.

Chinese Economic Area

The CEA is an informal reference to the economic integration of Southern China with Hong Kong and Taiwan which has proceeded without any "arrangement."

Chinese hedge

Applies mainly to convertible securities. Trading hedge in which one is short the convertible and long the underlying common, in the hope that the convertible's premium will fall. Antithesis of set-up.

Chinese wall

Communication barrier between financiers at a firm (investment bankers) and traders. This barrier is erected to prevent the sharing of inside information that bankers are likely to have.

CHIPS

See: Clearing House Interbank Payments System.

Choice market

Applies mainly to international equities. Locked market in London terminology.

Churning

Excessive trading of a client's account in order to increase the broker's commissions.

CI

The two-character ISO 3166 country code for COTE D'IVOIRE.

CIDA

See Canadian International Development Agency.

CIF

See: Cost Insurance and Freight.

Cincinnati Stock Exchange (CSE)

Stock exchange based in Cincinnati that is the only fully automated stock exchange in the US It has no trading floor, but handles all members' transactions using computers.

CIR

See Center for International Research.

Circle

Underwriters, actual or potential, often seek out and "circle" investor interest in a new issue before final pricing. The customer circled has basically made a commitment to purchase the issue if it is available at an agreed-upon price. If the actual price is other than that stipulated, the customer supposedly has first offer at the actual price.

Circuit breakers

Measures instituted by exchanges to stop trading temporarily when the market has fallen by a certain percentage in a specified period. They are intended to prevent a market free fall by permitting buy and sell orders to rebalance.

Circus swap

A fixed-rate currency swap against floating US dollar LIBOR payments.

Citizen bonds

Certificateless municipals that can be registered on stock exchanges and are listed in newspapers.

City code on takeovers and mergers

See: Dawn raid.

CK

The two-character ISO 3166 country code for COOK ISLANDS.

CL

The two-character ISO 3166 country code for CHILE.

Claim dilution

A decrease in the likelihood that one or more of a firm's claimants will be fully repaid, including time value of money considerations.

Claimant

A party to an explicit or implicit contract.

Class

In the case of derivative products, options of the same type-put or call-with the same underlying security. See: Series. In general, refers to a category of assets such as: domestic equity, fixed income, etc.

Class A/Class B shares

See: Classified stock.

Class action

A legal complaint filed by a lawyer or group of lawyers for a group of petitioners with an identical grievance, often with an award proportionate to the number of shareholders involved.

Classified Board

Also known as Staggered Board is one in which, the directors are placed into different classes and serve overlapping terms. Since only part of the board can be replaced each year, an outsider who gains control of a corporation may have to wait a few years before being able to gain control of the board. This slow replacement makes a classified board effectively delays takeovers. Sometimes known as a delay provision.

Classified stock

The division of stock into more than one class of common stock, usually called Class A and Class B. The specific features of each class, which are set out in the charter and bylaws, usually give certain advantages to the Class A shares, such as increased voting power.

"Class or Kind" of Merchandise

A term used in defining the scope of an antidumping investigation. Included in the "class or kind" of merchandize is merchandise sold in the home market which is "such or similar" to the petitioned product. "Such or similar" merchandise is that merchandise which is identical to or like the petitioned product in physical characteristics.

Class of Options

Option contracts of the smae type (call or put) and Style (American, European or Capped) that cover the same underlying security.

Claused Bill of Lading

A bill of lading whit a notation that indicates damage or shortage. Also called foul bill of lading and are the opposite of clean bills of lading.

Clawback

A dividend clawback is an arrangement whereby the equity owners commit to use dividends they have received in the past to finance the cash needs of the project or corporation in the future. Clawback has a more general definition. For example, premiums paid on an insurance policy may be refunded (or clawed back) if the policy is cancelled in a certain time frame. Such an arrangement is specified in the contract and referred to as a clawback provision.

Clean

In the context of general equities, block trade that matches buy or sell orders/interests, sparing the block trader any inventory risk (no net position and hence none available for additional customers). Natural. Antithesis of open.

Clean Bill of Lading

A receipt for goods issued by a carrier with an indication that the goods were received in "apparent good order and condition," without damages or other irregularities.

Clean Draft

A draft to which no documents have been attached.

Clean Float

Clean float refers to a system in which exchange rates are determined by market forces rather than government intervention or restrictions. See: Dirty Float.

Clean opinion

An auditor's opinion reflecting an unqualified acceptance of a company's financial statements.

Clean price

Bond price excluding accrued interest.

Clean Report of Findings

A report issued by an inspection firm, indicating that price has been verified, that the goods have been inspected prior to shipment, and that both conform to buyer specifications.

Clean up

In the context of general equities, purchase/sale of all the remaining supply of stock, or the last piece of a block, in a trade-leaving a net zero position.

"Clean your skirts"

In the context of general equities, "make all your obligated calls" check with all prior obligations in a security. Often preceded by "subject to."

Clear

To settle a trade is settled out by the seller delivering securities and the buyer delivering funds in the proper form. A trade that does not clear is said to fail. Comparison of the details of a transaction between broker/dealers prior to settlement; final exchange of securities for cash on delivery.

Clear a position

To eliminate a long or short position, leaving no ownership or obligation.

Clear title

Title to ownership that is untainted by any claims on the property or disputed interests, and therefore available for sale. This is usually checked through a title search by a title company.

Clearing corporations

Organizations that are affiliated with exchanges and are used to complete securities transactions by taking care of validation, delivery, and settlement.

Clearing House Automated Payments System (CHAPS)

A computerized clearing system for sterling funds that began operations in 1984. It includes 14 member banks, nearly 450 participating banks, and is one of the clearing companies within the structure of the Association for Payment Clearing Services (APACS).

Clearing House Electronic Subregister System (CHESS)

CHESS is the automatic transfer and settlement system for the majority of Australian Stock Exchange (ASX) listed securities.

Clearing house funds

Funds from the Federal Reserve System, requiring three days to clear, that are passed to and from banks.

Clearing House Interbank Payments System (CHIPS)

An international wire transfer system for high-value payments operated by a group of major banks.

Clearinghouse

An adjunct to a futures exchange through which transactions executed on its floor are settled by a process of matching purchases and sales. A clearing organization is also charged with the proper conduct of delivery procedures and the adequate financing of the entire operation.

Clearing member

A member firm of a clearing house. Each clearing member must also be a member of the exchange. Not all members of the exchange, however, are members of the clearing organization. All trades of a non-clearing member must be registered with, and eventually settled through, a clearing member.

Clearing Member Trade Agreement (CMTA)

An agreement that allows a client to execute derivative trades through different brokers yet consolidate positions for clearing purposes at one brokerage firm.

CLF

The ISO 4217 currency code for Chile Unidades de Fomento.

Clientele effect

Describes the tendary of funds or investments to be followed by groups of investors who have a similar preferences that the firm follow a particular financing policy, such as the amount of leverage it uses.

Clone fund

A new fund set up in a fund family to emulate another successful fund.

Close

The close is the period at the end of the trading session. Sometimes used to refer to closing price. Related: Opening.

Close a position

In the context of general equities, eliminate an investment from one's portfolio, by either selling a long position or covering a short position.

Close-end credit

An agreement in which advanced credit plus any finance charges are expected to be repaid in full over a definite time. Most real estate and automobile loans are closed-end agreements.

Close market

An active market in which there is a narrow spread between bid and offer prices, due to a high volume of trading and many competing market makers.

Closed corporation

A corporation whose shares are owned by just a few people, having no public market.

Closed-end management company

An investment company that has only a set number of shares of the mutual fund that it manages, and does not create new shares if demand increases. Antithesis of an open-end management company.

Closed-end fund

An investment company that sells shares like any other corporation and usually does not redeem its shares. A publicly traded fund sold on stock exchanges or over the counter that may trade above or below its net asset value. Related: Open-end fund.

Closed-end management company

An investment company that has only a set number of shares of the mutual fund that it manages, and does not create new shares if demand increases. Antithesis of an open-end management company.

Closed-end mortgage

Mortgage against which no additional debt may be issued.

Closed fund

A mutual fund that is no longer issuing shares, mainly because it has grown too large.

Closed out

Position that is liquidated when the client does not meet a margin call or cover a short sale.

Closely held

A corporation whose voting stock is owned by only a few shareholders.

Closely held company

A company who has a small group of controlling shareholders. In contrast, a widely-held firm has many shareholders. It is difficult or impossible to wage a proxy battle for any closely-held firm.

Closing costs

All the expenses involved in transferring ownership of real estate.

Closing price

Price of the last transaction of a particular stock completed during a day's trading session on an exchange.

Closing purchase

A transaction in which the purchaser's intention is to reduce or eliminate a short position in a stock, or in a given series of options.

Closing quote

The last bid and offer prices of a particular stock at the close of a day's trading session on an exchange.

Closing range

Also known as the range. The high and low prices, or bids and offers, recorded during the period designated as the official close. Related: Settlement price.

Closing sale

A transaction in which the seller's intention is to reduce or eliminate a long position in a stock, or a given series of options.

Closing tick

The net of the number of stocks whose closing prices are higher than their previous trades (uptick) against the number of stocks whose closing prices were lower than their previous trades (downtick). A positive closing tick indicates "buying at the close", or a bullish market; a negative closing tick indicates "selling at the close," or a bearish market. See: TRIN.

Closing transaction

Applies to derivative products. Buy or sell transaction that eliminates an existing position (selling a long option or buying back a short option). Antithesis of opening transaction.

Closing TRIN

See: TRIN.

Cloud on title

Any claim or encumbrance, usually discovered in a title search, that may impair the title to a property, and make its validity questionable. See: bad title.

CLP

The ISO 4217 currency code for Chilean Peso.

Club du Sahel

The Club du Sahel is an informal coalition which seeks to reverse the effects of drought and the desertification in the eight Sahelian zone countries: Burkina Faso, Chad, Gambia, Mali, Mauritania, Niger, Senegal, and the Cape Verde Islands. The Club coordinates plans and financing of aid and sustained economic development in the region. The Club (sometimes called "Club des Amis du Sahel"), formed in December 1975, comprises both donor countries (Austria, Belgium, Canada, France, the Netherlands, Switzerland, the United Kingdom, and the United States) and Sahelian zone countries. Headquarters are in Ouagadougou, Burkina Faso.

Cluster analysis

A statistical technique that identifies clusters of stocks whose returns are highly correlated within each cluster and relatively uncorrelated across clusters. Cluster analysis has identified groupings such as growth, cyclical, stable, and energy stocks.

CM

The two-character ISO 3166 country code for CAMEROON.

CMBS

See: Commercial Mortgage Backed Securities.

CME

See: Chicago Mercantile Exchange.

CML

See: Capital market line.

CMO

See: Collateralized mortgage obligation.

CMO REIT

A very risky type of Real Estate Investment Trust investing in the residual cash flows of Collateralized Mortgage Obligation (CMOs). CMO cash_flows are derived from the difference between the rates paid by the mortgage loan holders and the lower, shorter-term rates paid to CMO investors.

CMTA

See: Clearing Member Trade Agreement.

CN

The two-character ISO 3166 country code for CHINA.

CNY

The ISO 4217 currency code for Chinese Renminbi (Yuan).

CO

The two-character ISO 3166 country code for COLOMBIA.

Co-agent

An institution appointed by the issuer as co-transfer agent accepts and transfers certificates and sends daily activity journals to the primary record-keeping agent. A co-agent does not maintain security holder records, but is used to facilitate the transfer of stock in a geographic region not easily accessible to the issuer or its principal transfer agent.

Coattail investing

A risky trading practice of making trades similar to those of other successful investors, usually institutional investors.

CoCom

See Coordinating Committee on Multilateral Export Controls.

CoCom Cooperation Forum

The CCF provides a venue for emerging democracies in Central and Eastern Europe and the of the former Soviet Union to discuss international export controls and to help coordinate technical assistance efforts. The Forum, established in June 1992, held its first meeting in November 1992. At the close of 1992, 42 nations were CCF participants, including most states of the former Soviet Union (except Georgia, Tajikistan, and Turkmenistan) and all of the former Soviet satellites of Eastern and Central Europe (except the former Yugoslav republics).

Codex Alimentarius Commission

As a subsidiary body of the United Nations Food and Agricultural Organization and the World Health Organization, CAC (or CODEX) develops food standards and Recommended International Codes of Hygienic and/or Technological Practices. Commission standards are voluntary, becoming enforceable only if accepted as national standards. The Commission also works in cooperation with Regional Coordinating Committees (Africa, Europe, Latin America and the Caribbean) in promoting regional standards activities. The Commission was established in 1962; headquarters are in Rome, Italy.

COD transaction

See: Delivery versus payment.

Code of procedure

The guide of the National Association of Securities Dealers used to adjudicate complaints filed against NASD members.

Coefficient of determination

A measure of the goodness of fit of the relationship between the dependent and independent variables in a regression analysis; for instance, the percentage of variation in the return of an asset explained by the market portfolio return. Also known as R-square.

Coefficient of Variation

A measure of investment risk that defines risk as the standard deviation per unit of expected return.

Coffee, Sugar & Cocoa Exchange (CS&CE)

The New York-based commodity exchange trading futures and options. The CS&CE shares the trading floor at the Commodities Exchange Center.

Cofinancing agreements

Joint participation of the World Bank and other agencies or lenders in providing funds to developing countries.

Coherent Market Hypothesis

A hypothesis that the probability density function of the market may be determined by a combination of group sentiment and fundamental bias. Depending on combinations of these two factors, the market can be in one of four states: random walk, unstable transition, chaos, or coherence.

Coincident indicators

Economic indicators that give an indication of the status of the economy.

Coinsurance effect

Refers to the fact that the merger of two firms lessens the probability of default on either firm's debt.

Cold-calling

Calling potential new customers in the hope of selling stocks, bonds or other financial products and receiving commissions.

Collar

An upper and lower limit on the interest rate on a floating-rate note (FRN) or an adjustable-rate mortgage (ARM).

Collateral

Asset than can be repossessed if a borrower defaults.

Collateral trust bonds

A bond in which the issuer (often a holding company) grants investors a lien on stocks, notes, bonds, or other financial asset as security. Compare mortgage bond.

Collateralized Bond Obligation (CBO)

Investment-grade bonds backed by a collection of junk bonds with different levels of risk, called tiers, that are determined by the quality of junk bond involved. CBOs backed by highly risky junk bonds receive higher interest rates than other CBOs.

Collateralized mortgage obligation (CMO)

A security backed by a pool of pass-through rates , structured so that there are several classes of bondholders with varying maturities, called tranches. The principal payments from the underlying pool of pass-through securities are used to retire the bonds on a priority basis as specified in the prospectus. Related: mortgage pass-through security.

Collecting Bank

A bank that assists in obtaining payment in accordance with draft payment terms.

Collection

The presentation of a negotiable instrument for payment, or the conversion of any accounts receivable into cash.

Collection float

The period between the time is deposited a check in an account and the time funds are made available.

Collection fractions

The percentage of a given month's sales collected during the month of sale and each month following the month of sale.

Collection Papers

All documents (invoices, bills of lading, etc.) submitted to a buyer for the purpose of receiving payment for a shipment.

Collection period

See: Collection ratio.

Collection policy

Procedures a firm follows in attempting to collect accounts receivables.

Collection ratio

The ratio of a company's accounts receivable to its average daily sales, which gives the average number of days it takes the company to convert receivables into cash.

Collections System

The Collections System, a part of Customs' Automated Commercial System, controls and accounts for the billions of dollars in payments collected by Customs each year and the millions in refunds processed each year. Daily statements are prepared for the automated brokers who select this service. The Collections System permits electronic payments of the related duties and taxes through the Automated Clearinghouse capability. Automated collections also meet the needs of the importing community through acceptance of electronic funds transfers for deferred tax bills and receipt of electronic payments from lockbox operations for Customs bills and fees.

Collective wisdom

The combination of all the individual opinions about a stock's or security's value.

Colombo Plan

The Colombo Plan was established in 1951 to promote economic and social development among members in Asia and the Pacific. Members include: Afghanistan, Australia, Bangladesh, Bhutan, Burma, Cambodia, Canada, Fiji, India, Indonesia, Iran, Japan, South Korea, Laos, Malaysia, Maldives, Nepal, New Zealand, Pakistan, Papua New Guinea, Philippines, Singapore, Sri Lanka, Thailand, the United Kingdom, and the United States. The Plan's formal name is the Colombo Plan for Cooperative Economic Development in South and South-East Asia; headquarters are in Colombo, Sri Lanka.

Colombo Stock Exchange

Established in 1984, the only public stock exchange of Sri Lanka.

COLT (Continuous on-line trading system)

Computerized OTC traders assistance system that provides for trade entry and position monitoring, among other functions.

Comanager

A bank that ranks just below a lead manager in a syndicated Eurocredit or international bond issue. Comanagers may assist the lead manager bank in the pricing and issue of the instrument.

Combination

Applies to derivative products. Arrangement of options involving two long or two short positions with different expiration dates or strike (exercise) prices. See: Straddle.

Combination annuity

See: Hybrid annuity.

Combination bond +

A bond backed by the government unit issuing it as well as by revenue from the project that is to be financed by the bond.

Combination order

See: Alternative order

Combination matching

Also called horizon-matching, a variation of multiperiod immunization and cash flow-matching in which a portfolio is created that is always duration-matched and also cash-matched in the first few years.

Combination strategy

A strategy in which a put and call with the same strike price and expiration are either both bought or both sold. Related: Straddle

Combined financial statement

A financial statement that merges the assets, liabilities, net worth, and operating figures of two or more affiliated companies. A combined statement is distinguished from a consolidated financial statement of a company and subsidiaries, which must reconcile investment and capital accounts.

Come in

In the context of general equities, a fall in price.

Come out of the trade

In the context of general equities, trader's position in a security that results from executing a trade (or the expectations thereof). Antithesis of going into the trade.

Comeout

In the context of general equities, the opening. Antithesis of the close.

COMEX

A division of the New York Mercantile Exchange (NYMEX). Formerly known as the Commodity Exchange, COMEX is the leading US market for metals futures and options trading.

Comfort letter

A letter from an independent auditor in securities underwriting agreements to assure that information in the registration statement and prospectus is correctly prepared to the best of the auditor's knowledge.

Comision Panamericana de Normas Tecnicas

COPANT (English: Pan American Standards Commission) coordinates the activities of all institutes of standardization in the Latin American countries. The Commission develops all types of product standards, standardized test methods, terminology, and related matters. COPANT headquarters are in Buenos Aires, Argentina. U.S. contact with COPANT is maintained through the American National Standards Institute.

Comite Permanent Consultatif du Maghreb

The CPCM (English: Maghreb Permanent Consultative Committee) seeks to improve economic coordination among Maghreb countries, with eventual expectation of establishing a Maghreb economic community. Originally established in October 1964, the committee began operations in February 1966; its headquarters are in Tunis, Tunisia.

Commerce Business Daily

CBD is the Commerce Department's daily newspaper which lists government procurement invitations and contract awards, including foreign business opportunities and foreign government procurements.

Commerce Control List

The CCL includes all items — commodities, software, and technical data — subject to BXA export controls and incorporates not only the national security controlled items agreed to by CoCom (the "core" list), but also items controlled for foreign policy (i.e., biological warfare, nuclear proliferation, missile technology, regional stability, and crime control) and short supply. The list is divided into 10 general categories:

(1) materials,

(2) materials processing,

(3) electronics,

(4) computers,

(5) telecommunications and cryptography,

(6) sensors,

(7) avionics and navigation,

(8) marine technology,
(9) propulsion systems and transportation equipment, and
(10) miscellaneous.

Commercial Activity Report

The Commercial Activity Report, CAR, is prepared annually by the economic and commercial sections of the U.S. Embassies covering over 100 countries where the Department of Commerce is not represented. The CAR assesses the country's political, economic, and business activities, and market potential and strategies for increasing U.S. sales.

Commercial bank

Bank that offers broad range of deposit accounts, including checking, savings and time deposits and extends loans to individuals and business. Commercial banks can be contrasted with investment banking firms, such as brokerage firms, which generally are involved in arranging for the sale of corporate or municipal securities.

Commercial draft

Demand for payment.

Commercial hedgers

Companies that take futures positions in commodities so that they can guarantee prices at which they will buy raw materials or sell their products.

Commercial Information Management System

CIMS is a PC-based system used by International Trade Administration staff in export counseling. CIMS is a trade-related application using National Trade Data Bank CD-ROMs to disseminate market research and international economics data to US&FCS domestic offices and overseas posts. The system includes data on foreign traders and supports local collection and update of information on business contacts.

Commercial Invoice

The commercial invoice is a bill for the goods from the seller to the buyer. These invoices are often used by governments to determine the true value of goods for the assessment of customs duties and are also used to prepare consular documentation. Governments using the commercial invoice to control imports often specify its form, content, number of copies, language to be used, and other characteristics.

Commercial Law Development Program

The CLDP helps Central and Eastern Europe and the Baltic States develop a commercial infrastructure consistent with free market principles. The program, operated through the Commerce Department's International Trade Administration, is part of the U.S. Government's efforts to assist the region. CLPD is also compiling a Language Resources List of U.S. commercial law experts with strong language capabilities.

Commercial letters of credit

Trade-related agreement that a certain amount of bank funds is available to an entity.

Commercial loan

A short-term loan, typically 90 days, used by a company to finance seasonal working capital needs.

Commercial Mortgage Backed Securities

Similar to MBS but backed by loans secured with commercial rather than residential property. Commercial property includes multi-family, retail, office, etc., They are not standardized so there are a lot of details associated with structure, credit enhancement, diversification, etc., that need to be understood when valuing these instruments.

Commercial News USA

Commercial News USA, CNUSA, is an International Trade Administration (ITA) fee-based magazine, published 10 times per year. CNUSA provides exposure for U.S. products and services through an illustrated catalog and electronic bulletin boards. The catalog is distributed through U.S. Embassies and consulates to business readers in 155 countries. Copies are provided to international visitors at trade events around the world. The CNUSA program covers more than 30 industry categories. To be eligible, products must be at least 51 percent U.S. parts and 51 percent U.S. labor. The service helps U.S. firms identify potential export markets and make contacts leading to representation, distributorships, joint venture or licensing agreements, or direct sales.

Commercial Officers

Commercial officers are embassy officials who assist U.S. business through arranging appointments with local business and government officials, providing counsel on local trade regulations, laws, and customs; identifying importers, buyers, agents, distributors, and joint venture partners for U.S. firms; and other business assistance. At larger posts, International Trade Administration staff perform these functions. At smaller posts, commercial interests are represented by State's economic officers.

Commercial paper

Short-term unsecured promissory notes issued by a corporation. The maturity of commercial paper is typically less than 270 days; the most common maturity range is 30 to 50 days or less.

Commercial property

Real estate that produces some sort of income-producing property.

Commercial Risks

With respect to Eximbank guarantees, commercial risks cover nonpayment for reasons other than specified political risks. Examples are insolvency or protracted default. See also Political Risks.

Commercial Treaty

An agreement between two or more countries setting forth the conditions under which business between the countries may be transacted. May outline tariff privileges, terms on which property may be owned, the manner in which claims may be settled, etc.

Commingling

In the context of securities, this involves mixing customer-owned securities with brokerage firm-owned securities. This process is referred to as rehypothecation, which is the use of customers' collateral to secure their loans. This is legal with customer consent, although some securities and collateral must be kept separately.

Commission

The fee paid to a broker to execute a trade, based on number of shares, bonds, options, and/or their dollar value. In 1975, deregulation led to the establishment of discount brokers, who charge lower commissions than full service brokers. Full service brokers offer advice and usually have a staff of analysts who follow specific industries. Discount brokers simply execute a client's order and usually do not offer an opinion on a stock. Also known as a round-turn.

Commission broker

A broker on the floor of an exchange who acts as agent for a particular brokerage house and buys and sells stocks for the brokerage house on a commission basis.

Commission house

A firm that buys and sells futures contracts for customer accounts. Related: futures commission merchant, omnibus account.

Commission-only compensation

Payment to a financial adviser's of only commissions on investments purchased when the client implements the recommended financial plan.

Commitment

Describes a trader's obligation to accept or make delivery on a futures contract. Related: Open interest.

Commitment fee

A fee paid to a commercial bank in return for its legal commitment to lend funds that have not yet been advanced. Often used in risk arbitrage. Payment to institutional investors in the U.K. (pension funds and life insurance companies) by the lead underwriter of a takeover that takes place when the underwriter provides the target company's shareholders with a cash alternative for a target company's shares in exchange for the bidding companies' shares. The payment is typically 0.5% for the first 30 days, 1.25% for each week thereafter, and a final 0.75% acceptance payment when the takeover is completed.

Committee for the Implementation of Textile Agreements

CITA is an interagency committee chaired by the Department of Commerce which exercises the rights of the United States under the Multi-Fiber Arrangement.

CITA initiates "calls" for consultation when imports of a particular textile product from a particular country disrupt the U.S. domestic market for that product. Other member agencies include the Departments of Labor, State, and Treasury and the United States Trade Representative. See: Multi-Fiber Arrangement.

Committee of Experts

The CE is an autonomous body of 20 independent legal experts appointed by the International Labor Organization (ILO) Governing Body. The CE meets annually prior to the June conference to examine reports of governments on ILO conventions, and information provided by governments on what they have done with newly adopted conventions. The CE submits its report and findings to the International Labor Conference Committee on the Application of Conventions and Recommendations.

Committee on Renewable Energy, Commerce, and Trade

CORECT facilitates the cost-effective use of U.S. renewable energy products and services around the world. The Committee is comprised of 14 federal agencies: the Departments of Commerce, Defense, Energy, Interior, State, and Treasury, the Agency for International Development, Environmental Protection Agency, Export-Import Bank, Overseas Private Investment Corporation, Small Business Administration, Trade and Development Agency, United States Information Agency, and U.S. Trade Representative. The Committee, chaired by Energy, was established by legislation in 1984.

Committee on Trade and Development

The CTD was established in 1965 to consider how the General Agreement on Tariffs and Trade (GATT) can aid the economic development of Less Developed Country (LDC) contracting parties (that is, LDC members).

Committee on Foreign Investment in the United States

The Committee on Foreign Investment in the United States, CFIUS, was created in 1975 to provide guidance on arrangements with foreign governments for advance consultations on prospective major foreign governmental investments in the United States, and to consider proposals for new legislation or regulation relating to foreign investment. The authority was amended by Section 5021 (the Exon-Florio provision) of the Omnibus Trade and Competitiveness Act of 1988 (Section 721 of the Defense Production Act), which gives the President authority to review mergers, acquisitions, and takeovers of U.S. companies by foreign interests and to prohibit, suspend, or seek divestiture in the courts of investments that may lead to actions that threaten to impair the national security.

By Executive Order in December 1988, Treasury has authority to implement the Exon-Florio provision. CFIUS has 11 members: the Secretaries of the Treasury (the chair), State, Defense, and Commerce, the chairman of the Council of Economic Advisors, the U.S. Trade Representative, the Attorney General, the Director of the Office of Management and Budget, the Director of the Office of Science and Technology Policy, the Assistant to the President for National Security Affairs, and the Assistant to the President for Economic Policy.

The Assistant Secretary for Trade Development serves as Commerce's representative to CFIUS. The Commerce working group is chaired by the International Trade Administration and includes the Bureau of Export Administration, the Economics and Statistics Administration, the Technology Administration, and the Office of the General Counsel.

Committee on Uniform Securities Identification Procedures (CUSIP)

Committee that assigns identifying numbers and codes for all securities. These "CUSIP" numbers and symbols are used when recording all buy or sell orders.

Commodities Exchange Center (CEC)

The location of five New York futures exchanges: Commodity Exchange, Inc. (COMEX); the New York Mercantile Exchange (NYMEX); New York Cotton Exchange, Coffee, Sugar ;& Cocoa Exchange (CS;&CE), and New York Futures Exchange (NYFE).

Commodity

A commodity is food, metal, or another fixed physical substance that investors buy or sell, usually via futures contracts.

Commodity-backed bond

A bond with interest payments tied to the price of an underlying commodity.

Commodity Bundle

One unit of the collection of the complete set of goods produced and sold in the world market.

Commodity Channel Index

An index used in technical analysis. High values mean a potential future correction (downward movement in underlying asset) and low values potentially forecast a rally. Details in Donald Lambert's October 1980 article in *Commodities* Magazine.

Commodity Credit Corporation

The CCC finances a variety of federal domestic and international farm programs, including Title I, Title II, and Title III of Public Law 480 (Food for Peace). The CCC is a government-owned and operated corporation within the U.S. Department of Agriculture (USDA), and is managed by a board of directors headed by the Secretrary of Agriculture. All members of the board and the corporation's officers and staff are officials of USDA. The CCC provides financing and stability to the marketing and exporting of agricultural commodities.

Commodity futures contract

An agreement to buy a specific amount of a commodity at a specified price on a particular date in the future, allowing a producer to guarantee the price of a product or raw material used in production.

Commodity Futures Trading Commission (CFTC)

An agency created by the US Congress in 1974 to regulate exchange trading in futures.

Commodity Import Programs

CIPs finance the export of U.S. goods to U.S.-aid recipient countries. Under CIPs, the Agency for International Development (AID) makes dollars available to the assisted country on a loan or grant basis to pay for essential commodity imports. In nearly all cases, these imports come from the United States. CIPs are used to provide relatively fast disbursing balance of payments support or to generate local currency for budget support for project goals, particularly in efforts designed to encourage private sector development. CIP agreements usually provide for AID's financing of a wide variety of basic items including agricultural goods, construction and transportation equipment, fertilizer, chemicals, raw materials, semi-finished products, and foodstuffs. CIPs do not finance military or police equipment, luxury items, or items of questionable safety or efficacy. In some cases, the range of allowable commodities is narrowed in order to tailor them to development needs of particular sectors in the assisted country or to accomplish other, specific development goals.

Commodity indices

Indices measuring the price and performance of physical commodities, often by the price of futures contracts for the commodities that are listed on commodity exchanges.

Commodity Jurisdiction

Export jurisdiction of products is administered by the State Department's Office of Defense Trade Controls (DTC) if the commodities are defense articles, technical data, and services or by the Commerce Department's Bureau of Export Administration if the commodities are dual-use items. An exporter may request DTC to conduct a commodity jurisdiction (CJ) review if the exporter is uncertain as to whether an item is covered by the United States Munitions List (USML) or believes it has been inappropriately placed on the list. CJ procedures include deadlines for making a determination and the use of criteria assessing: (a) performance, (b) significant military or intelligence applicability, and (c) significant civilian applicability.

Commodity paper

A loan or advance secured by commodities.

Commodity Research Bureau

Produces a popular price index of 17 commodities which is often used to track inflationary trends in the economy.

Commodity Trading Advisor

An investment manager that focuses on long and short trading in the futures markets. The trades are often intraday trades. Sometimes referred to as Managed Futures.

Common Agricultural Policy

The CAP is a set of regulations by which members states of the European Community (EC) seek to merge their individual agricultural programs into a unified effort to promote regional agricultural development, fair and rising standards of living for the farm population, stable agricultural markets, increased agricultural productivity, and methods of dealing with food supply security. Two of the principal elements of the CAP are the variable levy (an import duty amounting to the difference between EC target farm prices and the lowest available market prices of imported agricultural commodities) and export restitutions, or subsidies, to promote exports of farm goods that cannot be sold within the EC at the target prices.

Common-base-year analysis

The representing of accounting information over multiple years as percentages of amounts in an initial year.

Common code

A nine-digit identification code issued jointly by CEDEL and Euroclear. As of January 1991 common codes replaced the earlier separate CEDEL and Euroclear codes.

Common External Tariff

A uniform tariff adopted by a customs union to be assessed on imports entering the union territory from countries outside the union; abbreviated: CET or CXT.

Common factor

An element of return that influences many assets. According to multiple factor risk models, the common factors determine correlations between asset returns. Common factors include size (often measured by market capitalization), valuation measures such as price to book value ratio and dividend yield, industries and risk indices.

Common Market

A common market (as opposed to a free trade area) has a common external tariff and may allow for labor mobility and common economic policies among the participating nations. The European Community is the most notable example of a common market.

Common Monetary Agreement

South Africa, Lesotho, and Swaziland are members of the CMA under which they apply uniform exchange control regulations to ensure monetary order in the region. Funds are freely transferable among the three countries, and Lesotho and Swaziland have free access to South African capital markets. Lesotho also uses the South African currency, the rand. The CMA was formed in 1986 as a result of the renegotiation of the Rand Monetary Agreement (RMA) which was originally formed in 1974 by the same member countries.

Common shares

In general, a public corporation has two types of shares, common and preferred. The common shares usually entitle the shareholders to vote at shareholders meetings. The common shares have a discretionary dividend.

Common-size analysis

The representing of balance sheet items as percentages of assets and of income statement items as percentages of sales.

Common-size statement

A statement in which all items are expressed as a percentage of a base figure, useful for purposes of analyzing trends and changing relationship among financial statement items. For example, all items in each year's income statement could be presented as a percentage of net sales.

Common Standard Level of Effective Protection

The common standard level of effective protection, CSP, refers to the minimum shared standards between the U.S. and CoCom members for implementing an effective export control system, including licensing and enforcement elements.

Common stock

Securities that represent equity ownership in a company. Common shares let an investor vote on such matters as the election of directors. They also give the holder a share in a company's profits via dividend payments or the capital appreciation of the security. Units of ownership of a public corporation with junior status to the claims of secured/unsecured creditors, bondholders and preferred shareholders in the event of liquidation.

Common stock equivalent

A convertible security that is traded like an equity issue because the optioned common stock is trading at a high price.

Common stock fund

A mutual fund investing only in common stock.

Common stock market

The market for trading equities, not including preferred stock.

Common stock/other equity

Value of outstanding common shares at par, plus accumulated retained earnings. Also called shareholders' equity.

Common stock ratios

Ratios that are designed to measure the relative claims of stockholders to earnings (cash flow per share), and equity (book value per share) of a firm.

Commonwealth

A commonwealth is a free association of sovereign independent states that has no charter, treaty, or constitution. The association promotes cooperation, consultation, and mutual assistance among members. The British Commonwealth (with headquarters in London, England) is the most notable example; it included 50 states at the beginning of 1991.

Commonwealth Development Corporation

The CDC is a British public corporation which provides medium- and long-term loans and equity financing for development-related private and public sector projects in selected countries. CDC financing is available for projects in the following sectors: agriculture (livestock, horticulture, and acquaculture), forestry, fishing, mineral extraction, industry, public utilities, transport, telecommunications, low-cost housing, hotels, construction and civil engineering, financial management and consultancy services, and leasing of assets. The Corporation does not invest in schools, colleges, hospitals, public service works or broadcasting. Since 1969, CDC has been able to invest in non-Commonwealth countries with ministerial agreement. The CDC was established in 1948; headquarters are in London, England.

Commonwealth of Independent States

The CIS was established in December 1991 as an association of 11 republics of the former Soviet Union. The members include: Russia, Ukraine, Belarus (formerly Byelorussia), Moldova (formerly Moldavia), Armenia, Azerbaijan, Uzbekistan, Turkmenistan, Tajikistan, Kazakhstan, and Kirgizstan (formerly Kirghiziya). The Baltic states did not join. Georgia maintained observer status, before joining the CIS in November 1993. Until that time, the NIS (Newly Independent States) differed from the CIS in that the NIS is a collective reference to 12 Soviet republics, including Georgia.

Communautes Europeenes

The CE mark is applied to products, their packaging or paperwork as a declaration of conformity, third party testing and/or certification, quality assurance audit and/or full type approval by a body authorized by a European Economic Community member state and recognized by the European Commission. Effective January 1, 1993, the CE mark on a product attests that it complies with all in-force Directives pertinent to it. The CE mark preempts all other European Community national safety marks. If it is discovered that the CE mark has been improperly affixed, the product in question will be prohibited and no longer marketed. Legal penalties are at the discretion of each member state.

Communications Satellite Corporation

COMSAT was established in 1963 under provision of the Communications Satellite Act of 1962. The legislation directed that COMSAT establish the world's first commercial international satellite communications system. The Act also stipulated that the company operate as a shareholder-owned "for-profit" corporation. COMSAT represents the U.S. in the International Telecommunications Satellite Organization.

Community Reinvestment Act (CRA)

Enacted by Congress in 1977, the CRA encourages banks to help meet the credit needs of their communities for housing and other purposes, particularly in neighborhoods with low or moderate incomes, while maintaining safe and sound operations.

Compagnie Francaise d'Assurance pour le Commerce Exterieur

COFACE is a French company acting as a commercial export finance agency by insuring short-term political and commercial risk and by facilitating the financing for export credit. Any French exporter (manufacturers, intermediaries, confirmers, and merchants) of French goods and services can be insured for sales abroad. In conjunction with the Banque Fran‡aise du Commerce Exterieur and other banks and institutions, COFACE provides services similar to the Export-Import Bank. COFACE was established in 1946; headquarters are in Paris, France.

Companion bonds

A class of a Collateralized Mortgage Obligation (CMO) whose principal is paid off first when the underlying mortgages are prepaid due to falling interest rates. When interest rates rise, there will be lower prepayments of the principal; companion bonds therefore absorb most of the prepayment risk of a CMO.

Company

A proprietorship, partnership, corporation, or other form of enterprise that engages in business.

Company doctor

An executive, usually appointed from outside, brought in to turn a company around and make it profitable.

Company-specific risk

Related: Unsystematic risk.

Comparative advantage

Theory suggesting that specialization by countries can increase worldwide production.

Comparative credit analysis

Comparing a firm to others that have a desired target debt rating in order to deduce an appropriate financial ratio target.

Comparative statements

Financial statements for different periods, that allow the comparison of figures to illustrate trends in a company's performance.

Comparison

Short for "comparison ticket," a memorandum between two brokers that confirms the details of a transaction to be carried out.

Comparison universe

A group of money managers of similar investment style used to assess relative performance of a portfolio manager.

Compensating balance

An excess balance that is left in a bank to provide indirect compensation for loans extended or services provided.

Compensation

Arrangement under which the delivery of goods to a party is paid for by buying back a certain amount of the product from the recipient of the goods.

Compensatory and Contingency Financing Facility

The CCFF is an International Monetary Fund (IMF) facility which provides resources to an IMF member for a shortfall in export earnings or an excess in cereal import costs that is due to factors largely beyond the member's control and which is temporary. Compensatory financing, introduced in 1963 and broadened several times, provides aid to members experiencing balance of payments problems as a result of fluctuations in commodity prices and shortfalls of receipts in tourism, "workers' remittances" and most services. Contingency financing helps members with IMF-supported adjustment programs to maintain the momentum of adjustment efforts in the face of a broad range of unanticipated, adverse external shocks — for example, changes in international interest rates or prices or primary imports or exports.

Compensatory Financing Facility (CFF)

Entity that attempts to reduce the impact of export instability on country economies.

Competence

Sufficient ability or fitness for one's needs. The necessary abilities to be qualified to achieve a certain goal or complete a project.

Competition

Intra- or intermarket rivalry between or among businesses trying to obtain a larger piece of the same market share.

Competition ahead

Often used in risk arbitrage. Situation whereby another OTC market maker has transacted with investment bank at the stated market level before the bid/offer has been made.

Competitive bidders

One of two categories of bidders on Treasury securities: competitive and noncompetitive. Competitive bidders are usually financial institutions.

Competitive bidding

A securities offering process in which securities firms submit competing bids to the issuer for the securities the issuer wishes to sell.

Competitive offering

An offering of securities through competitive bidding.

Complete

In the context of general equities, to fill an order.

Complete capital market

A market in which there is a distinctive marketable security for each and every possible outcome.

Complete portfolio

The entire portfolio, including risky and risk-free assets.

Completion bonding

Insurance that a construction contract will be completed successfully.

Completion risk

The risk that a project will not be brought into operation successfully.

Completion undertaking

An undertaking either (1) to complete a project so that it meets certain specified performance criteria on or before a certain specified date, or (2) to repay project debt if the completion test cannot be met.

Complexity Theory

The theory that processes with a large number of seemingly independent agents can spontaneously organize themselves into a coherent system.

Compliance department

A department in all organized stock exchanges to ensure that all companies, traders, and brokerage firms comply with Securities and Exchange Commission and exchange rules and regulations.

Composite Currency Peg

See Exchange Rate Classifications.

Composite tape

See: Tape.

Composite Theoretical Performance

Computer hardware export license requirements are evaluated according to Composite Theoretical Performance (CTP), which replaced the former Processing Data Rate (PDR) parameter. CTP is measured in Million Theoretical Operations Per Second (MTOPS). CTP was developed by the U.S. as a new parameter, and was adopted by CoCom during the Core List negotiations, because PDR was not applicable to certain modern computer architectures such as vector processors, massively parallel processors, and array processors. CTP is designed to measure all of these architectures, as well as signal processing equipment.

Composition

Voluntary arrangement to restructure a firm's debt, under which payment is reduced.

Compound Annual Growth Rate

Best defined by example. If you invest $100 today and make 5% in the first year and reinvest ($105) and make 8% in the second year, the compound annual growth rate is 6.489%. The calculation is $100x1.05x1.08 = $113.4 which is what you end up with at the end of year two. The average return is [square root(113.4/

100) -1]= 0.06489 or 6.489%. Note 1. If we had three compounding periods we would take the cubic root (power of 1/3). Note 2. If we had invested at exactly 6.489 in both periods, we get $100x1.06489x1.06489 = $113.4. Note 3. The example is directed to a return - but CAGR could be applied to earnings growth, GDP growth, etc.

Compound Annual Return

See: Compound Annual Growth Rate.

Compound growth rate

See: Compound Annual Growth Rate.

Compound interest

Interest paid on previously earned interest as well as on the principal.

Compound option

Option on an option.

Compounding

The process of accumulating the time value of money forward in time. For example, interest earned in one period earns additional interest during each subsequent time period.

Compounding frequency

The number of compounding periods in a year. For example, quarterly compounding has a compounding frequency of 4.

Compounding period

The length of the time period that elapses before interest compounds (a quarter in the case of quarterly compounding).

Comprehensive due diligence investigation

The investigation of a firm's business in conjunction with a securities offering to determine whether the firm's business and financial situation and its prospects are adequately disclosed in the prospectus for the offering.

Comprehensive Income

Comprehensive income is the change in equity of a business enterprise during a period from transactions and other events from non-owner sources. It includes all non-owner changes in equity (in contrast to net income which does not include some changes in equity). Financial Accounting Standards Board (FASB) issued the Statement of Financial Accounting Standards No. 130 (SFAS 130), *Reporting Comprehensive Income*. For fiscal years beginning after December 15, 1997, SFAS 130 requires the disclosure of both net income and a more 'comprehensive' measure of income which includes four items recorded as owners' equity under previous FASB pronouncements: adjustments to unrealized gains and losses on available-for-sale marketable securities (SFAS 115), foreign currency translation adjustments (SFAS 52), minimum required pension liability adjustments (SFAS 87), and changes in the market values of certain futures contracts qualifying as hedges (SFAS 80).

COMPRO

COMPRO is an on-line trade data retrieval system maintained by the International Trade Administration within the U.S. Department of Commerce. The system is exclusively for use within the federal government trade community (ITA, USTR, ITC, and other executive branch agencies. It is also the oldest and best known component of the Trade Policy Information System (TPIS). COMPRO is slated to be replaced in the FY 1995-96 TPIS modernization, but its functions will remain available in an expanded and generalized form. See: Trade Policy Information System.

Comptroller

The corporate manager responsible for the firm's accounting activities. Sometimes referred to as the contoller (which means the same thing).

Comptroller of the Currency

A government official, appointed by the president, who keeps control over all national banks, and receives reports from the banks at least quarterly, to be published in newspapers.

Computerized market timing system

A computer system that compiles large amounts of trading data in search of patterns and trends to make buy and sell recommendations.

Concave

Property that a curve is below a straight line connecting two end points. If the curve falls above the straight line, it is called convexity.

Concentration account

A single centralized account into which funds collected at regional locations (lockboxes) are transferred.

Concentration Banks

A small number of large banks a firm contracts with to periodically collect the firm's deposit balances from a group of smaller banks.

Concentration services

Movement of cash from different lockbox locations into a single concentration account from which disbursements and investments are made.

Concession

The per-share or per-bond compensation of a selling group for participating in a corporate underwriting.

Concession agreement

An understanding between a company and the host government that specifies the rules under which the company can operate locally.

Conditional call

Applies mainly to convertible securities. Circumstances under which a company can effect an earlier call, usually stated as percentage of a stock's trading price during a particular period, such as 140% of the exercise price during a 40-day trading span.

Conditional call options

A protective guarantee that, in the event a high yield bond is called, the issuing corporation will replace the bond with a noncallable bond of the same life and terms as the bond that is being called.

Conditional sales contracts

Similar to equipment trust certificates, except that the lender is either the equipment manufacturer or a bank or finance company to which the manufacturer has sold the conditional sales contract.

Condor

Applies to derivative products. Option strategy consisting of both puts and calls at different strike prices to capitalize on a narrow range of volatility. The payoff diagram takes the shape of a bird.

Conduit theory

A theory that because investment companies are merely conduits for capital gains, dividends, and interest, which are in fact passed through to shareholders, the investment company should not be taxed at the corporate level.

Confédération Internationale du Crédit Agricole (COCA)

COCA (English: International Confederation of Agricultural Credit, ICAC) coordinates documentation and information improvements pertaining to agricultural credit. Confederation members are agricultural credit banks and other institutions which provide or study agricultural credits. ICAC was established in 1932; headquarters are in Zurich, Switzerland.

Conférence Européenne des Administrations des Postes et des Télécommunications (CEPT)

CEPT (English: European Conference of Postal and Telecommunications Administration) harmonizes, simplifies, and improves postal and telecommunications services. Many CEPT standards creating activities have been assumed by the European Telecommunications Standards Institute. CEPT maintains offices in Paris, France and Bern, Switzerland. See European Telecommunications Standards Institute.

Conference on Security and Cooperation in Europe (CSCE)

CSCE was established in 1991 as a successor to the Eastern bloc's Council for Mutual Economic Assistance (CMEA or COMECON). CSCE administers residual tariffs and quotas and relations with other organizations.

Confidence indicator

A measure of investors' faith in the economy and the securities market. A low or deteriorating level of confidence is considered by many technical analysts as a bearish sign.

Confidence letter

Statement by an investment bank that it is highly confident that the financing for its client/acquirer's takeover can and will be obtained. Often used in risk arbitrage.

Confidence level

In risk analysis, the degree of assurance that a specified failure rate is not exceeded.

Confirmation

The written statement that follows any "trade" in the securities markets. Confirmation is issued immediately after a trade is executed. It spells out settlement date, terms, commission, etc.

Confirmed Letter of Credit

A letter of credit which a bank other than the bank that opened it agrees to honor as though they had themselves issued it. This additional confirmation is in addition to the obligation of the bank which issued the letter of credit.

Confirming Bank

The bank which has confirmed a letter of credit opened by another bank.

Confirming

Confirming is a financial service in which an independent company confirms an export order in the seller's country and makes payment for the goods in the currency of that country. Among the items eligible for confirmation (and thereby eligible for credit terms) are the goods themselves, inland, air, and ocean transportation cost, forwarding fees, custom brokerage fees, and duties .For the exporter, confirming means that the entire export transaction from plant to end-user can be fully coordinated and paid for over time. Confirming is common in Europe, however, it is still in its infancy in the United States.

Confirming Order

A purchase order placed verbally or otherwise for goods or services prior to the formal issuance of a purchase document against authorized encumbered funds.

"Confirm me out"

Used for listed equity securities. "Go to the floor and check with the specialist or floor broker that my previously active order has been canceled and was not executed". One does not have to honor any trade reported after given a "firm out".

Conflict between bondholders and stockholders

Bondholders and stockholders may have interests in a corporation that conflict. Sources of conflict include dividends, distortion of investment, and underinvestment. Protective covenants in bond documents work to resolve these conflicts.

Conforming loans

Mortgage loans that meet the qualifications of Freddie Mac or Fannie Mae, which are bought from lenders and issued as pass-through securities.

Conformité Europėene

The CE mark signifies that a product meets specific EC-wide conformity assessment requirements. The mark does not endorse the quality or durability of a product, but only that it satisfies mandatory technical requirements. The designation is needed for sale of products which become subject to Community-wide "new-approach" directives. See: European Norm.

Conglomerate

A firm engaged in two or more unrelated businesses.

Conglomerate merger

A merger involving two or more firms that are in unrelated businesses.

Conseil de Coopé,ration Douanière

See: Customs Cooperation Council.

Conseil de l'Entente

The Conseil de l'Entente (Entente Council) is an alliance of Benin, Burkina Faso, Côte d'Ivoire, Niger (all formerly part of French West Africa), and Togo (which joined in 1966). The Council was established in 1959; headquarters are in Abidjan, Côte d'Ivoire.

Consensus forecast

The mean of all financial analysts' forecasts for a company.

Consignee

The person, fir m or representative to whom a seller or shipper sends merchandise and who, upon presentation of the necessary documents, is recognized as owner of the merchandise for the purpose of the declaration and payment of customs [illegible] his term also is used as applying to one to whom g[illegible]s are shipped, usually the shipper's risk, when an outright sale has not been made.

Consignment

Delivery of merchandise from an exporter (the consignor) to an agent (the consignee) under agreement that the agent sell the merchandise for the account of the exporter. The consignor retains title to the goods until the consignee has sold them. The consignee sells the goods for commission and remits the net proceeds to the consignor.

Consol

A government bond with no maturity . Popular in Great Britain. The formula for valuing these bonds is simple. The consol payment divided by yield to maturity is the price of the bond.

Consolidated financial statement

A financial statement that shows all the assets, liabilities, and operating accounts of a parent company and its subsidiaries.

Consolidated mortgage bond

A bond that covers several units of property, sometimes refinancing mortgages on the properties.

Consolidated tape

Used for listed equity securities. Combined ticker tapes of the NYSE and the curb. Network A covers the NYSE-listed securities and is used to identify the originating market. Network B does the same for AMEX-listed securities and also reports on securities listed on regional stock exchanges. See: tape.

Consolidated tax return

A tax return combining the reports of affiliated companies, that are at least 80% owned by a parent company.

Consolidation

The Consolidation Endorsement may be added to an Open Cargo Policy at an agreed premium, to provide coverage on merchandise while in transit to, and while at, a common consolidation point for the purpose of preparing or consolidating the merchandise for export. Uniting into one unit or body. There is consolidation when a new operating company is formed from the merger of two or more existing companies that contribute their assets and then lose their own respective legal identities.

Consolidation loan

A loan that is used to combine and finance payments on other loans.

Consortia of American Businesses in Eastern Europe

The CABEE program, administered by the U.S. Department of Commerce, provides grants of up to $500,000 to each of five non-profit consortia of for-profit companies to cover up to one-half of costs of starting-up commercial operations in Eastern Europe. Launched under the American Business and Private-Sector Development Initiative for Eastern Europe, CABEE is intended to help overcome difficulties faced by small and medium-sized firms in entering Eastern Europe markets. CABEE was established in June 1991.

Consortia of American Businesses in the Newly Independent States

CABNIS is a cooperative, cost-sharing program of government and the private sector that helps non-profit business consortia establish a commercial presence and pursue business in the Newly Independent States on behalf of profit-making U.S. corporations and associations. The program provides matching government grants of up to $500,000 to each consortia. CABNIS, established in July 1992, is administered by the Commerce Department's International Trade Administration. CABNIS was established in July 1992.

Consortium

A group of companies that cooperate and share resources in order to achieve a common objective.

Consortium banks

A merchant banking subsidiary set up by several banks that may or may not be of the same nationality. Consortium banks are common in the Euromarket and are active in loan syndication.

Constant-dollar plan

Method of purchasing securities by investing a fixed amount of money at set intervals. The investor buys more shares when the price is low and fewer shares when the price is high, thus reducing the overall cost.

Constant Dollars

Values adjusted to a base price level, calculated by dividing current dollars by a price deflator. Use of constant dollars eliminates the effects of price inflation and permits the comparison of output volumes over time. Also known as "real" dollars.

Constant-growth model

Also called the Gordon-Shapiro model, an application of the dividend discount model that assumes (1) a fixed growth rate for future dividends, and (2) a single discount rate.

Constant ratio plan

Maintaining a predetermined ratio between stock and fixed income investments through regular adjustments of distribution of funds into different investments. See: formula investing.

Constant yield method

Allocation of annual interest on a zero-coupon security for income tax use.

Constructed Value

A means of determining fair or foreign market value when sales of such or similar merchandise do not exist or, for various reasons, cannot be used for comparison purposes. The "constructed value" consists of the cost of materials and fabrication or other processing employed in producing the merchandise, general expenses of not less than 10 percent of material and fabrication costs, and profit of not less than 8 percent of the sum of the production costs and general expenses. To this amount is added the cost of packing for exportation to the United States. See: Tariff Act of 1930.

Construction loan

A short-term loan to finance building costs.

Constructive receipt

The date a taxpayer receives dividends or other income, for use in the determination of taxes.

Consul

A government official residing in a foreign country who is charged with the representation of the interests of his country and its nationals.

Consular Declaration

A formal statement, made to the consul of a foreign country, describing goods to be shipped.

Consular Documents

Bills of lading, certificates of origin or special invoice forms that are officially signed by the consul of the country of destination.

Consular Information Sheet

See: Travel Advisory Program.

Consular Invoice

A document, required by some foreign countries, describing a shipment of goods and showing information such as the consignor, consignee, and value of the shipment. Certified by a consular official of the foreign country, it is used by the country's customs officials to verify the value, quantity, and nature of the shipment.

Consultative Committee for International Telephone and Telegraphy

CCITT facilitates U.S. coordination of communications standards issues. CCITT is a part of the International Telecommunications Union (ITU), which is an international treaty organization. The State Department is responsible for coordinating and presenting U.S. positions to the ITU. See: International Telecommunications Union.

Consultative Group on International Agricultural Research

CGIAR, an informal association of public and private sector donors, supports international agricultural research centers (IARCs) around the world. The centers develop new ways to increase sustainable food production and improve the nutritional and economic well-being of low-income people. CGIAR, sponsored by the World Bank and other international organizations, was established in 1971; its Secretariat is in Washington, D.C. The research centers include:

— Centro Internacional de Agricultura Tropical (CIAT), Colombia

— Centro Internacional de Mejoramiento de Maizy Trigo (CIMMYT), Mexico

— International Board for Plant Genetic Resources (IBPGR), Italy

— International Center for Agricultural Research in Dry Areas (ICARDA), Syria

— International Centre for Research in Forestry (ICRAF), Kenya

— International Crops Research Institute for the Semi-Arid Tropics (ICRISAT), India
— International Food Policy Research Institute (IFPRI), United States
— International Irrigation Management Institute (IIMI), Sri Lanka
— International Institute of Tropical Agriculture (IITA), Nigeria
— International Livestock Center for Africa (ILCA), Ethiopia
— International Laboratory for Research on Animal Diseases (ILRAD), Kenya
— International Network for the Improvement of Banana and Plantain (INIBAP), France
— International Rice Research Institute (IRRI), Philippines
— International Service for National Agricultural Research (ISNAR), Netherlands and
— West Africa Rice Development Association (WARDA), Côte d'Ivoire.

Consumer Advisory Council (CAC)

A statutory body established by Congress in 1976. The Council, with 30 members who represent a broad range of consumer and creditor interests, advises the Federal Reserve Board on the exercise of its responsibilities under the Consumer Credit Protection Act and on other matters on which the Board seeks its advice.

Consumer credit

Credit a firm grants to consumers for the purchase of goods or services. Also called retail credit.

Consumer Credit Protection Act of 1968

Federal legislation establishing rules for the disclosure of the terms of a loan to protect borrowers. See: Truth in lending.

Consumer debenture

An investment note issued directly to the public by a financial institution.

Consumer durables

Consumer products that are expected to last three years or more, such as an automobile or a home appliance.

Consumer finance company

See: Finance company.

Consumer goods

Goods not used in production but, bought for personal or household use such as food, clothing, and entertainment.

Consumer interest

Interest paid on consumer loans; e.g., interest on credit cards and retail purchases.

Consumer Price Index

The CPI, as it is called, measures the prices of consumer goods and services and is a measure of the pace of US inflation. The US Department of Labor publishes the CPI every month.

Consumption tax

See: Value-added tax.

Contadora Group

The Contadora Group, which first met on the Panamanian island of Contadora in January 1983, seeks solutions to conflict in Central America. Members include the foreign ministers of Colombia, Mexico, Panama, and Venezuela. Group headquarters are in Mexico City, Mexico.

Contagion

Excess correlation of equity or bond returns. For example, under usual conditions we might observe a certain level of correlation of market returns. A period of contagion would be associated with much higher-than-expected correlation. Some examples are the conjectured contagion in East Asian markets beginning in July 1997 when the Thai currency devalued and the impact across many emerging markets of the Russian default.

Contagion is difficult to identify because you need some sort of measure of the expected correlation. It is complicated because correlation's are known to change through time, for example, see Erb, Harvey and Viskanta's article in the 1994 Financial Analysts Journal. In periods of negative returns, correlation's (and volatility) are known to increase, so what might appear to be excessive may not be contagion.

Container

A uniform, sealed, reusable metal "box" in which merchandise is shipped by vessel, truck, or rail. Standard lengths include 10, 20, 30, and 40 feet (40 foot lengths are generally able to hold about 40,000 pounds). Containers of 45 and 48 feet are also used, as well as containers for shipment by air.

Containerization

Shipping systems based on large cargo-carrying containers ranging up to 48 feet long that can be easily interchanged between trucks, trains and ships without rehandling the contents.

Contango

A market condition in which futures prices are higher in the distant delivery months.

Contingency graph

A plot of the net profit to a speculator in currency options under various exchange rate scenarios.

Contingency order

In the context of general equities, order to buy one security, if the trader can sell another, usually given that certain price limits or conditions reach a certain level. Swap, switch order.

Contingent claim

A claim that can be made only if one or more specified outcomes occur.

Contingent deferred sales charge (CDSC)

The formal name for the load of a back-end load fund.

Contingent immunization

An arrangement in which the money manager pursues an active bond portfolio strategy until an adverse investment experience drives the then-available potential return down to the safety net level. When that point is reached, the money manager is obligated to pursue an immunization strategy to lock in the safety-net level return.

Contingent order

An order which can be executed only if another event occurs; i.e. "sell Oct 45 call 7-1/4 with stock 52 or lower".

Contingent pension liability

Under ERISA, a firm is liable to its pension plan participants for up to 39% of the net worth of the firm.

Contingent Voting Power

Enables preferred stockholders to vote when the company fails to satisfy the agreement between itself and the preferred stockholders.

Continuous compounding

The process of accumulating the time value of money forward in time on a continuous, or instantaneous, basis. Interest is earned constantly, and at each instant, the interest that accrues immediately begins earning interest on itself.

Continuous net settlement (CNS)

Method of securities clearing and settlement using a clearing house, which matches transactions to securities available, resulting in one net receive or deliver position at the end of the day.

Continuous random variable

A random value that can take any fractional value within specified ranges, as contrasted with a discrete variable.

Contraband

During the time of war, materials carried aboard a vessel that could aid a belligerent in the process of the war, such as arms, weapons or munitions.

Contra broker

The broker on the buy side of a sell order or the sell side of a buy order.

Contract

A term of reference describing a unit of trading for a financial or commodity future. Also, the actual bilateral agreement between the buyer and seller of a transaction as defined by an exchange.

Contracting Parties

Contracting parties are the signatory countries to the GATT. These countries have accepted the specified obligations and privileges of the GATT agreement.

Contract month

The month in which futures contracts may be satisfied by making or accepting a delivery.

Contractual Claim

An amount that by legal agreement must be paid periodically to the buyer of a security; contractual claim may also specify the time at which the principal must be repaid and other details.

Contractual Intermediary

Holder of an indirect claim in through a legal agreement that specifies that the individual must make periodic, fixed payments to the intermediary in exchange for the right to receive payments from the intermediary in the future.

Contractual plan

A plan in which fixed dollar amounts of mutual fund shares are purchased through periodic investments, usually featuring some sort of additional incentive for the fixed period payments.

Contramarket stock

In the context of general equities, stock that tends to go against the trend of the market as a whole, such as a commodities-related stock or one in an industry out of favor with investors in a bull market.

Contrarian

An investment style that leads one to buy assets that have performed poorly and sell assets that have performed well. There are two possible reasons this strategy might work. The first is a mean-reversion argument; that is, if the asset has deviated from its usual level, it should eventually return to that usual level. The second reason has to do with overreaction. Investors might have overreacted to bad news sending the asset price lower than it should be.

Contrarian investing

Ignoring market trends by buying securities that the investor considers undervalued and out of favor with other investors.

Contributed capital

See: Paid-in capital.

Contribution

Money placed in an individual retirement account (IRA), an employer-sponsored retirement plan, or other retirement plan for a particular tax year. Contributions may be deductible or nondeductible, depending on the type of account.

Contribution margin

The difference between variable revenue and variable cost.

Control

50% of the outstanding votes plus one vote.

Control Limits

The upper and lower limits on the acceptable level of cash that minimizes the sum of the opportunity cost of excessive cash and the cost of marketable security transactions.

Control parameters

In a nonlinear dynamic system, the coefficient of the order parameter; the determinant of the influence of the order parameter on the total system. See: Order Parameter.

Control person

See: Affiliated person.

Control-share Acquisition Laws

See Supermajority.

Control stock

The shares owned by the controlling shareholders of a corporation.

Controlled commodities

Commodities regulated by the Commodities Exchange Act of 1936 in order to prevent fraud and manipulation in commodities futures markets.

Controlled disbursement

A service that provides for a single presentation of checks each day (typically in the early part of the day).

Controlled foreign corporation (CFC)

A foreign corporation whose voting stock is more than 50% owned by US stockholders, each of whom owns at least 10% of the voting power.

Controller

The corporate manager responsible for the firm's accounting activities. Sometimes referred to as the comptroller (which means the same thing).

Convenience yield

The extra advantage that firms derive from holding the commodity rather than a future position.

Convention

See: International Agreements.

Conventional Arms Transfer

The transfer of non-nuclear weapons, aircraft, equipment, and military services from supplier states to recipient states. U.S. arms are transferred by grants as in the Military Assistance Program (MAP); by private commercial sales; and by government-to-government sales under Foreign Military Sales (FMS). MAP provides defense articles and defense services to eligible foreign governments on a grant basis.

FMS provides credits and loan repayment guarantees to enable eligible foreign governments to purchase defense articles and defense services.

Conventional mortgage

A loan based on the credit of the borrower and on the collateral for the mortgage.

Conventional option

An option contract arranged off the trading floor and not traded regularly.

Conventional pass-throughs

Also called private-label pass-throughs, any mortgage pass-through security not guaranteed by government agencies. Compare agency pass-throughs.

Conventional project

A project with a negative initial cash flow (cash outflow), which is expected to be followed by one or more future positive cash flows (cash inflows).

Convention on Contracts for the International Sale of Goods

The UN Convention on Contracts for the International Sale of Goods, CISG, became the law of the United States in January 1988. CISG establishes uniform legal rules governing formation of international sales contracts and the rights and obligations of the buyer and seller. The CISG applies automatically to all contracts for the sale of goods between traders from two different countries that have both ratified the CISG, unless the parties to the contract expressly exclude all or part of the CISG or expressly stipulate a law other than the CISG.

Convention statement

An annual statement filed by a life insurance company in each state where it does business in compliance with that state's regulations. The statement and supporting documents show, among other things, the assets, liabilities, and surplus of the reporting company.

Convergence

The movement of the price of a futures contract toward the price of the underlying cash commodity. At the start, the contract price is higher because of time value. But as the contract nears expiration, and time value decreases, the futures price and the cash price converge.

Conversion

In the context of securities, refers to the exchange of a convertible security such as a bond into stock.

In the context of mutual funds, refers to the free exchange of mutual fund shares from one fund to another in a single family.

Conversion factors

Rules set by the Chicago Board of Trade for determining the invoice price of each acceptable deliverable Treasury issue against the Treasury Bond futures contract.

Conversion feature

Specification of the right to transform a particular investment to another form of investment, such as switching between mutual funds or converting preferred stock or bonds to common stock.

Conversion parity

See: Market conversion price.

Conversion parity price

Related: Market conversion price.

Conversion parity/value

Applies mainly to convertible securities. Common stock price at which a convertible bond can become exchangeable for common shares of equal value; value of a convertible bond based solely on the market value of the underlying equity. Par value + conversion ratio. See bond value, investment value, parity.

Conversion Period

The time period during which an investor can exchange a convertible security for common stock.

Conversion premium

The extent by which the conversion price of a convertible security exceeds the prevailing common stock price at the time the convertible security is issued.

Conversion price

Applies mainly to convertible securities. Dollar value at which convertible bonds, debentures, or preferred stock can be converted into common stock, as specified when the convertible is issued.

Conversion ratio

Applies mainly to convertible securities. Relationship that determines how many shares of common stock will be received in exchange for each convertible bond or preferred stock when a conversion takes place. It is determined at the time of issue and is expressed either as a ratio or as a conversion price from which the ratio can be figured by dividing the par value of the convertible by the conversion price.

Conversion value

The value of a convertible security if it is converted immediately. Also called parity value.

Converted put

See Synthetic Put.

Convertibility

The ability to exchange a currency without government restrictions or controls.

Convertible adjustable preferred stock (Caps)

The interest rate on caps is adjustable and is pegged to Treasury security rates. They can be exchanged at par value for common stock or cash after the next period's dividend rates are revealed.

Convertible arbitrage

A practice, usually of buying a convertible bond and shorting a percentage of the equivalent underlying common shares, to create a positive cash flow position (with expected returns above the riskless rate) in a static environment and benefits from capital appreciation should the convertible's premium rise. This form of investing is far from riskless and requires constant monitoring. See: Chinese hedge and setup

Convertible bond

General debt obligation of a corporation that can be exchanged for a set number of common shares of the issuing corporation at a prestated conversion price.

Convertible Currency

A currency that can be bought and sold for other currencies at will.

Convertible eurobond

A eurobond that can be converted into another asset, often through exercise of attached warrants.

Convertible exchangeable preferred stock

Convertible preferred stock that may be exchanged, at the issuer's option, into convertible bonds that have the same conversion features as the convertible preferred stock.

Convertible 100

Goldman Sachs index of the 100 convertibles of greatest institutional importance. Weighted by issue size, it measures the performance of its components against that of their underlying common stock and against other broad market indexs as well.

Convertible preferred stock

Preferred stock that can be converted into common stock at the option of the holder. See also: participating convertible preferred stock.

Convertible price

The contractually specified price per share at which a convertible security can be converted into shares of common stock.

Convertible security

A security that can be converted into common stock at the option of the securityholder; includes convertible bonds and convertible preferred stock.

Convex

Curved, as in the shape of the outside of a circle. Usually referring to the price/required yield relationship for option-free bonds.

Convexity

Property that a curve is above a straight line connecting two end points. If the curve falls below the straight line, it is called concave.

Cook the books

To deliberately falsify the financial statements of a company. This is an illegal practice.

Cooling-off period

The period of time between the filing of a preliminary prospectus with the Securities and Exchange Commission and the actual public offering of the securities.

Cooperative

An organization owned by its members. Examples are agriculture cooperatives that assist farmers in selling their products more efficiently and apartment buildings owned by the residents who have full control of the property.

Cooperative Contracts

Any agreement to engage in joint economic activities, such as a contract for an enterprise owned and operated by one or all of the parties who use its facilities or services. Simple oral and written contracts may be used by companies to begin a cooperative working relationship in an international strategic alliance. Contract terms, conditions and covenants may be brief and should encourage close cooperation between the companies involved for a reasonable time period, to enable their personnel to learn more about each other's capabilities and goals before they consider moving into an even closer more complicated and formal alliance.

Cooperator Program

See: Foreign Market Development Program.

Coordination Council for North American Affairs

The CCNAA, the counterpart to the American Institute in Taiwan, unofficially represents Taiwan's interests in the United States. The Council provides information on trade, business, and investment opportunities to the American business community. Council headquarters are in Washington, D.C. See: American Institute in Taiwan.

COP

The ISO 4217 currency code for Colombian Peso.

Copenhagen Stock Exchange

The only securities exchange in Denmark. It features electronic trading of stocks, bonds, futures, and options.

Coproduction

Coproduction is a U.S. government program implemented either by a government-to-government arrangement or through specific licensing arrangements by designated commercial firms. These programs enable foreign entities to acquire the know-how to manufacture or assemble, repair, maintain, and operate all or part of a specific defense item or weapon, communication, or support system.

Core capital

The capital required of a thrift institution, which must be at least 2% of assets to meet the rules of the Federal Home Loan Bank.

Core List

National security controls are based largely on CoCom's international industrial list (known generally as the "core list"), which replaced the old industrial list effective September 1991. The core list includes items in ten categories: (1) materials, (2) materials processing, (3) electronics, (4) computers, (5) telecommunications and cryptography, (6) sensors, (7) avionics and navigation, (8) marine technology, (9) propulsion systems and transportation equipment, and (10) miscellaneous.

Core competence

Primary area of expertise. Narrowly defined fields or tasks at which a company or business excels. Primary areas of specialty.

Cornering the market

Purchasing a security or commodity in such volume as to achieve control over its price. An illegal practice.

Corporate acquisition

The acquisition of one firm by another firm.

Corporate bonds

Debt obligations issued by corporations.

Corporate charter

A legal document creating a corporation.

Corporate equivalent yield

A comparison of the after-tax yield of government bonds selling at a discount and corporate bonds selling at par.

Corporate finance

One of the three areas of the discipline of finance. It deals with the operation of the firm (both the investment decision and the financing decision) from the firm's point of view.

Corporate financial management

The application of financial principles within a corporation to create and maintain value through decision-making and proper resource management.

Corporate financial planning

Financial planning conducted by a firm that encompasses preparation of both long-and short-term financial plans.

Corporate financing committee

A committee of the NASD that reviews underwriters' SEC-required documents to ensure that proposed markups are fair and in the public interest.

Corporate income fund (CIF)

A unit investment trust featuring a fixed portfolio of high-grade securities and other investments, usually with monthly distribution of income.

Corporate processing float

The time that elapses between receipt of payment from a customer and the deposit of the customer's check in the firm's bank account; the time required to process customer payments.

Corporate repurchase

Active buying by a corporation of its own stock in the marketplace. Reasons for repurchase include putting idle cash to use, raising EPS, creating support for a stock price, increasing internal control (shark repellant), or stock for ESOP or pension plans. Repurchase is subject to rules, such as that buying must be on a zero minus or a minus tick, after the opening and before 3:30 p.m.

Corporate tax view

The argument that double (corporate and individual) taxation of equity returns makes debt a cheaper financing method.

Corporate taxable equivalent

Rate of return required on a par bond to produce the same after-tax yield to maturity that the quoted premium or discount bond would generate.

Corporate Trust

The function of servicing and maintaining records for debt securities issued by a corporation.

Corporation

A legal entity that is separate and distinct from its owners. A corporation is allowed to own assets, incur liabilities, and sell securities, among other things.

C Corporation

A corporation that elects to be taxed as a corporation. The C corporation pays federal and state income taxes on earnings. When the earnings are distributed to the shareholders as dividends, this income is subject to another round of taxation (shareholder's income). Essentially, the C corporations' earnings are taxed twice. In contrast, the S corporation's earnings are taxed only once.

Corporacion Andina de Fomento

See: Andean Group.

Corpus

See: Principal.

Correction

Reverse movement, usually downward, in the price of an individual stock, bond, commodity, or index. If prices have been rising on the market as a whole, and then fall dramatically, this is know as a correction within an upward trend. Antithesis of a technical rally. See: Dip, break.

Correlation

Statistical measure of the degree to which the movements of two variables (stock/option/convertible prices or returns) are related. See: Correlation coefficient.

Correlation coefficient

A standardized statistical measure of the dependence of two random variables, defined as the covariance divided by the standard deviations of two variables.

Correlation Dimension

An estimate of the Fractal Dimension which measures the probability that two points chosen at random will be within a certain distance of each other, and examines how this probability changes as the distance is increased. White noise will fill its space since its components are uncorrelated, and its correlation dimension is equal to whatever dimension it is placed in. A dependent system will be held together by its correlations and retain its dimension whatever embedding dimension it is placed in, as long as it is greater than its fractal dimension.

Correlation Integral

The probability that two points are within a certain distance from one another. Used in the calculation of the correlation dimension.

Correspondent

A financial organization that performs services (acts as an intermediary) in a market for another organization that does not have access to that market.

Correspondent bank

Bank that accepts deposits of, and performs services for, another bank (called a respondent bank); in most cases, the two banks are in different cities.

Cosigner

A term referring to a person, other than the principal borrower, who signs for a loan. The cosigner(s) assumes equal liability for the loan.

Cost

The opposite of revenue. An expense that reflects the price of purchasing goods, services and financial instruments. A cash cost means that cash is given up today to the purchase.

Cost accounting

A branch of accounting that provides information to help the management of a firm evaluate production costs and efficiency.

Cost and Freight (CFR)

Seller is responsible for the payment of freight to carry goods to a named destination, as agreed with the buyer. This should be used with ocean shipments only, as the point where risk and responsibility pass from seller to buyer is the rail of the carrying vessel.

Cost basis

The original price of an asset, used to determine capital gains.

Cost-benefit ratio

The net present value of an investment divided by the investment's initial cost. Also called the profitability index.

Cost of capital

The required return for a capital budgeting project.

Cost of carry

Out-of-pocket costs incurred while an investor has an investment position. Examples include interest on long positions in margin account, dividend lost on short margin positions, and incidental expenses. Related: Net financing cost.

Cost-of-carry market

Applies to derivative products. Futures contracts trade in a "cost-of-carry market" where the underlying commodity can be stored, insured, and converted into the future easily and inexpensively. Arbitrageurs, because of the ease of switching from the spot commodity to futures, will keep these markets in line with prevailing interest rates.

Cost company arrangement

Arrangement whereby the shareholders of a project receive output free of charge but agree to pay all operating and financing charges of the project.

Cost of equity

The required rate of return for an investment of 100% equity.

Cost and Freight

Cost and Freight (CFR) to a named overseas port of import. Under this term, the seller quotes a price for the goods that includes the cost of transportation to the named point of debarkation. The cost of insurance is left to the buyer's account. (Typically used for ocean shipments only. CPT, or carriage paid to, is a term used for shipment by modes other than water.) Also, a method of import valuation that includes insurance and freight charges with the merchandise values.

Cost of funds

Interest rate associated with borrowing money.

Cost of goods sold

The total cost of buying raw materials, and paying for all the factors that go into producing finished goods.

Cost Insurance and Freight (CIF)

Seller is responsible for the payment of freight to carry goods to a named destination, as agreed with the buyer. The seller is also responsible for providing cargo insurance at minimum coverage against the buyer's risk of loss or damage to the goods during transport. This term should be used with ocean shipments only, as the point where risk and responsibility pass from seller to buyer is the rail of the carrying vessel.

Cost of lease financing

A lease's internal rate of return.

Cost of limited partner capital

The discount rate that equates the after-tax inflows with outflows for capital raised from limited partners.

Costs of Manufacture

In the context of dumping investigations, the costs of manufacture, COM, is equal to the sum of the materials, labor and both direct and indirect factory overhead expenses required to produce the merchandise under investigation.

"Cost me"

Refers to over-the-counter trading. "The price I must pay to obtain the securities you wish to buy is [$]". Usually, a standard markup (1/8) is then applied for resale to this buyer. Antithesis of can get.

Cost-plus contract

A contract in which the selling price is based on the total cost of production plus a fixed percentage or fixed amount.

Cost of Production

A term used to refer to the sum of the cost of materials, fabrication and/or other processing employed in producing the merchandise sold in a home market or to a third country together with appropriate allocations of general administrative and selling expenses. COP is based on the producer's actual experience and does not include any mandatory minimum general expense or profit as in "constructed value." See: Tariff Act of 1930.

Cost-push inflation

Inflation caused by rising prices, usually from increased raw material or labor costs that push up the costs of production. Related: Demand-pull inflation.

Cost records

The records maintained by an investor of the prices at which securities transactions are made, so that capital gains can be computed.

Cost Recovery Period

The number of years it takes to fully depreciate a capital asset. This time period is based on classification of the depreciable life of an asset.

Cottonseed Oil Assistance Program

COAP, one of four export subsidy programs operated by the Department of Agriculture, helps U.S. exporters meet prevailing world prices for cottonseed oil in targeted markets. USDA pays cash to U.S. exporters as bonuses, making up the difference between the higher U.S. cost of acquiring cottonseed oil and the lower world price at which it is sold.

Council of American States in Europe

This Council is composed of state representatives resident in Europe supportive of official U.S. promotions.

Council of Economic Advisers

A group of economists appointed by the President of the United States to provide economic counsel and help prepare the president's budget presentation to Congress.

Council of Economic Arab Unity

CEAU fosters economic integration among Arab nations. The Council's activities compiling statistics, conducting research, and promoting a customs union. The

Council was established in 1964; headquarters are in Amman, Jordan. The Council oversees the Arab Common Market, which comprises Egypt, Iraq, Jordan, Libya, Mauritania, Syria, and Yemen.

Council of Europe

The COE (also: CE; French: Conseil de l'Europe)) was established in May 1949 to encourage unity and social and economic growth among members, which currently include: Austria, Belgium, Cyprus, Denmark, Finland, France, Germany, Greece, Hungary, Iceland, Ireland, Italy, Liechtenstein, Luxembourg, Malta, the Netherlands, Norway, Portugal, San Marino, Spain, Sweden, Switzerland, Turkey, and the United Kingdom. COE headquarters are in Strasbourg, France.

Council for Mutual Economic Assistance

The Council for Mutual Economic Assistance, CMEA or COMECON, was established in 1949 ostensibly to create a common market. CMEA was a Soviet initiative with Bulgaria, Czechoslovakia, Hungary, Poland, and Romania as founder members. The Council was later joined by the German Democratic Republic, Mongolia, Cuba, and Vietnam; Yugoslavia held associate status. Members normally received some products, particularly oil and gas, from the former Soviet Union at below-market prices. CMEA was succeeded in 1991 by the Organization for Economic Cooperation (OIEC).

Council on Security and Cooperation in Europe

Members include: Albania, Armenia, Austria, Azerbaijan, Belgium, Bulgaria, Byelarus, Canada, Cyprus, Czechoslovakia, Denmark, Estonia, Finland, France, Germany, Greece, the Holy See, Hungary, Iceland, Ireland, Italy, Kazakhstan, Kyrgyzstan, Latvia, Liechtenstein, Lithuania, Luxembourg, Malta, Moldova, Monaco, Netherlands, Norway, Poland, Portugal, Romania, Russia, San Marino, Spain, Sweden, Switzerland, Tajikistan, Turkey, Turkmenistan, Ukraine, the United Kingdom, the United States, Uzbekistan, and Yugoslavia.

Countercyclical stocks

Stocks whose price tends to rise when the economy is in recession or the market is bearish, and vice versa.

Counter trade

The exchange of goods for other goods rather than for cash; barter.

Counterpart items

In the balance of payments, counterpart items are analogous to unrequited transfers in the current account. They arise through the double-entry system in balance of payments accounting and refer to adjustments in reserves owing to monetization or demonetization of gold, allocation or cancellation of SDRs, and revaluation of the various components of total reserves.

Counterparties

The parties to an interest rate swap.

Counterparty

Party on the other side of a trade or transaction.

Counterparty risk

The risk that the other party to an agreement will default. In an options contract, the risk to the option buyer that the option writer will not buy or sell the underlying as agreed.

Counterpurchase

Exchange of goods between two parties under two distinct contracts expressed in monetary terms.

Countertrade

Countertrade is an umbrella term for several sorts of trade in which the seller is required to accept goods, services, or other instruments or trade, in partial or whole payment for its products. Forms include barter, buy-back or compensation, offset requirements, swap, switch, or triangular trade, evidence or bilateral clearing accounts. Some include offsets as a form of countertrade; others make a distinction based on the view that countertrade is a reciprocal exchange of goods and services used to alleviate foreign exchange shortages of importers and that offsets are used as a means for advancing industrial development objectives and may include equity investments.

In counterpurchase (one of the most common forms of countertrade), exporters agree to purchase a quantity of goods from a country in exchange for that country's purchase of the exporter's product. The goods being sold by each party are typically unrelated but may be equivalent in value.

In a compensation or buy-back deal, exporters of heavy equipment, technology, or even entire facilities agree to purchase a certain percentage of the output of the facility.

Barter is a simple swap of one good for another. Switch trading is a complicated form of barter, involving a chain of buyers and sellers in different markets. See: Offsets.

Countertrade Ratio

Percent of the value of the original export that is offset by counterdeliveries.

Countervailing Duty

An extra charge that a country places on imported goods to counter the subsidies or bounties granted to the exporters of the goods by their home governments. The duty is allowed by the Code on Subsidies and Countervailing Duties negotiated at the Tokyo Round, if the importing country can prove that the subsidy would cause injury to domestic industry. U.S. countervailing duties can only be imposed after the International Trade Commission has determined that the imports are causing or threatening to cause material injury to a U.S. industry.

Country allocations

The percentages of a fund's net assets distributed to securities of various countries. These percentages serve as an indicator of a fund's diversification and its vulnerability to fluctuations in foreign financial markets or currency exchange rates.

Country beta

Covariance of a national economy's rate of return and the rate of return of the world economy divided by the variance of the world economy.

Country diversification

Investment of a global or international portfolio's assets in securities of various countries.

Country economic risk

Developments in a national economy that can affect the outcome of an international financial transaction.

Country of Export Destination

Country of destination for exports is the country where the goods are to be consumed, further processed, or manufactured, as known to the shipper at the time of exportation. If the shipper does not know the country of ultimate destination, the shipment is credited to the last country to which the shipper knows that the merchandise will be shipped in the same form as when exported.

Country financial risk

Centers around the ability of a national economy to generate enough foreign exchange to meet payments of interest and principal on its foreign debt.

Country Groups

For export control purposes, the Bureau of Export Administration of the U.S. Commerce Department separates countries into seven country groups designated by the symbols: Q, S, T, V, W, Y, Z. Canada and Antartica are not included in any country group. Canada is referred to by name throughout the Export Administration Regulations. Antartica is controlled according to the country that occupies the area in Antartica where the items proposed for export or re-export will be used. See: Export Control Classification Number.

Country of Origin

The U.S. Customs Service defines country of origin as the country where an article was wholly grown, manufactured or produced, or, if not wholly grown, cultivated or produced in one country, the last country in which the article underwent a substantial transformation. Duty rates vary according to the country of origin.

Country risk

General level of political, financial, and economic uncertainty in a country which impacts the value of the country's bonds and equities.

Country selection

A type of active international management that measures the contribution to performance attributable to investing in the better-performing stock markets of the world.

Coupon

The periodic interest payment made to the bondholders during the life of the bond.

Coupon bond

A bond featuring coupons that must be presented to the issuer in order to receive interest payments.

Coupon-equivalent rate

See: Equivalent bond yield.

Coupon equivalent yield

True interest cost expressed on the basis of a 365-day year.

Coupon pass

Canvassing by the desk of primary dealers to determine the inventory and maturities of their Treasury securities. The desk then decides whether to buy or sell certain issues (coupons) in order to add or withdraw reserves.

Coupon payments

A bond's interest payments.

Coupon rate

In bonds, notes, or other fixed income securities, the stated percentage rate of interest, usually paid twice a year.

Court of International Trade

The CIT has jurisdiction over any civil action against the United States arising from Federal laws governing import transactions. The court hears antidumping, product classification, and countervailing duty matters as well as appeals of unfair trade practice cases from the International Trade Commission. The court was originally established in 1890; principal offices are located in New York City, but the court is empowered to hear and determine cases arising at any port or place within the jurisdiction of the United States. The judges are appointed for life by the President, subject to Senate confirmation.

Covariance

A statistical measure of the degree to which random variables move together. A positive covariance implies that one variable is above (below) its mean value when the other variable is above (below) its mean value.

Covenants

Provisions in a bond indenture or preferred stock agreement that require the bond or preferred stock issuer to take certain specified actions (affirmative covenants) or to refrain from taking certain specified actions (negative covenants).

Cover

The purchase of a contract to offset a previously established short position.

Coverage

See: Fixed-charge coverage.

Coverage initiated

Usually refers to the fact that analysts begin following a particular security. This usually happens when there is enough trading in it to warrant attention by the investment community.

Coverage ratios

Ratios used to test the adequacy of cash flows generated through earnings for purposes of meeting debt and lease obligations, including the interest coverage ratio and the fixed-charge coverage ratio.

Covered

A written option is considered to be covered if the writer also has an opposing market position on a share-for-share basis in the underlying security. That is, a short call is covered if the underlying stock is owned, and a short put is covered (for margin purposes) if the underlying stock is also short in the account. In addition, a short call is covered if the account is also long another call on the same security, with a striking price equal to or less than the striking price of the short call. A short put is covered if there is also a long put in the account with a striking price equal to or greater than the striking price of the short put.

Covered call

A short call option position in which the writer owns the number of shares of the underlying stock represented by the option contracts. Covered calls generally limit the risk the writer takes because the stock does not have to be bought at the market price, if the holder of that option decides to exercise it.

Covered call writing strategy

A strategy that involves writing a call option on securities that the investor owns. See: Covered or hedge option strategies.

Covered foreign currency loan

A loan denominated in a currency other than that of the borrower's home country, for which repayment terms are prearranged through the use of a forward currency contract.

Covered interest arbitrage

Occurs when a portfolio manager invests dollars in an instrument denominated in a foreign currency and hedges the resulting foreign exchange risk by selling the proceeds of the investment forward for dollars.

Covered Interest Rate Parity

The principle that the yields from interest-bearing foreign and domestic investments should be equal when the forward currency market is used to predetermine the domestic currency payoff from a foreign investment.

Covered or hedge option strategies

Strategies that involve a position in an option as well as a position in the underlying stock, designed so that one position will help offset any unfavorable price movement in the other, including covered call writing and protective put buying. Related: Naked strategies

Covered option

Option position that is offset by an equal and opposite position in the underlying security. Antithesis of naked option.

Covered position

Use of an option in a trading strategy in the underlying asset is already owned.

Covered put

A put option position in which the option writer also is short the corresponding stock or has deposited, in a cash account, cash or cash equivalents equal to the exercise of the option. This limits the option writer's risk because money or stock is already set aside. In the event that the holder of the put option decides to exercise the option, the writer's risk is more limited than it would be on an uncovered or naked put option.

Covered straddle

An option strategy in which one call and one put with the same strike price and expiration are written against 100 shares of the underlying stock. In actually, this is not a "covered" strategy because asignment on the short put would require purchase of stock on margin. This method is also know as a covered combination.

Covered straddle write

The term used to describe the strategy in which an investor owns the underlying security and also writes a straddle on that security. This is not really a covered position.

Covered writer

An investor who writes options only on stock that he or she owns, so that option positions may be collected.

Covering

Using forward currency contracts to predetermine the domestic currency amount of an expected future foreign receipt or payment.

CPI

A measure of inflation. See: Consumer Price Index.

CPT

See: Carriage Paid To.

CR

The two-character ISO 3166 country code for COSTA RICA.

Cramdown

The ability of the bankruptcy court to confirm a plan of reorganization over the objections of some classes of creditors.

Cram-down deal

A merger in which stockholders are forced to accept undesirable terms, such as junk bonds instead of cash or equity, due to the absence of any better alternatives.

Crash

Dramatic loss in market value. The last great crash was in 1929. Some refer to October 1987 as a crash but the market return was positive.

Crawling peg

An automatic system for revising the exchange rate. It involves establishing a par value around which the rate can vary up to a given percent. The par value is revised regularly according to a formula determined by the authorities.

Crawling Peg System

The crawling peg is a procedure in which a currency exchange rate is altered frequently (multiple times a year), generally to adjust for rapid inflation. Between changes, the exchange rate for the currency remains fixed. See: Exchange Rate Classifications.

CRB

See: Commodity Research Bureau.

CRC

The ISO 4217 currency code for Costa Rican Colon.

Credible signal

A signal that provides accurate information; a signal that can distinguish among senders.

Credit

Money loaned.

Credit analysis

Evaluating information on companies and bond issues in order to estimate the ability of the issuer to live up to its future contractual obligations. Related: Default risk.

Credit balance

The surplus in a cash account with a broker after purchases have been paid for, plus the extra cash from the sale of securities.

Credit bureau

An agency that researches the credit history of consumers so that creditors can make decisions about granting of loans.

Credit card

Any card, plate or coupon book that may be used repeatedly to borrow money or buy goods and services on credit.

Credit for Countertrade/Offsets

Procedure that reduces the size of the countertrade/ offset commitment of a primary supplier on the basis of prescribed or approved commercial initiatives that the primary supplier and/or its designated agents undertake. Decisions related to the approval and the amount of countertrade/offset credit to be granted to the primary supplier rests with special government agencies that are responsible for monitoring the supplier's performance.

Credit history

A record of how a person has borrowed and repaid debt.

Credit enhancement

Purchase of the financial guarantee of a large insurance company to raise funds.

Crediting rate

The interest rate offered on an investment type insurance policy.

Credit insurance

Insurance against abnormal losses due to unpaid accounts receivable.

Credit linked security

A note whose cash flow depends upon a credit event or credit measure of a referenced entity or asset such as default, credit spread, or rating change. The manager would purchase such a note to hedge against possible down grades, or loan defaults that would guarantee payment into the portfolio of the manager even if moneys on referenced assets are reduced.

Creditor

Lender of money.

Creditor's committee

A group representing firms that have claims on a company facing bankruptcy or extreme financial difficulty.

Credit period

The length of time for which a firm's customer is granted credit.

Credit Policy Delay

The period between the sale of goods for a credit and the payment for those goods. This lag is determined largely by the selling firm's credit policy.

Credit quality

A measure of a bond issuer's ability to repay interest and principal in a timely manner. Rating agencies assign letter designations such as AAA, AA, and so forth. The lower the rating, the higher the probability of default.

Credit rating

An evaluation of an individual's or company's ability to repay obligations or its likelihood of not defaulting See: Creditworthiness.

Credit Rating Agencies

Firms that compile information on and issue public credit ratings for a large number of companies.

Credit risk

The risk that an issuer of debt securities or a borrower may default on its obligations, or that the payment may not be made on a negotiable instrument. Related: Default risk.

Credit Risk Insurance

Insurance designed to cover risks of nonpayment for delivered goods. See also Marine insurance.

Credit scoring

A statistical technique that combines several financial characteristics to form a single score to represent a customer's creditworthiness.

Credit spread

Applies to derivative products. Difference in the value of two options, when the value of the one sold exceeds the value of the one bought. One sells a "credit spread." Antithesis of a debit spread Related: Quality spread.

Credit Standards

The guidelines a company follows to determine whether a credit applicant is creditworthy.

Credit Terms

The conditions under which credit will be extended to a customer. The components of credit terms are: cash discount, credit period, net period.

Credit Tranches

The credit tranche policy is the International Monetary Fund's (IMF) basic policy on the use of its general resources. Credit is made available in four tranches, each equivalent to 25 percent of a member's quota.

A first credit tranche purchase raises the IMF's holdings of the purchasing member's currency to no more than 25 percent of quota. Generally, a member may request use of the IMF's resources in the first credit tranche if it demonstrates that it is making reasonable efforts to overcome its balance of payments difficulties. Also, a member may request use of the first credit tranche as part of a stand-by arrangement.

Subsequent purchases are made in the upper credit tranches. These resources are made available if a member adopts policies that provide appropriate grounds for expecting that the member's balance of payments difficulties will be resolved within a reasonable period. Use of these resources is almost always made under a stand-by or an extended arrangement. See: International Monetary Fund.

Credit union

A not-for-profit institution that is operated as a cooperative and offers financial services such as low-interest loans, to its members.

Credit watch

A warning by a bond rating firm indicating that a company's credit rating may change after the current review is concluded.

Creditworthiness

Eligibility of an individual or firm to borrow money.

Creeping tender offer

The process by which a group attempting to circumvent certain provisions of the Williams Act gradually acquires shares of a target company in the open market.

CREST

CREST is CrestCo's real-time settlement system for UK and Irish shares and other corporate securities. CrestCo has provided settlement systems for government bonds and money market instruments in the UK since 1990.

Crisp Sets

The fuzzy set term for traditional set theory. That is, an object either belongs to a set, or does not.

Critical Circumstances

A determination made by the Assistant Secretary for Import Administration (of the Commerce Department's International Trade Administration) as to whether there is a reasonable basis to believe or suspect that there is a history of dumping in the United States or elsewhere of the merchandise under consideration, or that the importer knew or should have known that the exporter was selling this merchandise at less than fair value, and there have been massive imports of this merchandise over a relatively short period. This determination is made if an allegation of critical circumstances is received from the petitioner. See: Tariff Act of 1930.

Critical Levels

Values of control parameters where the nature of a nonlinear dynamic system changes. The system can bifurcate, or make the transition from stable to turbulent behavior. An example is the straw that breaks the camel's back.

Currency Swaps

See: Swaps.

Cross

Securities transaction in which the same broker acts as agent for both sides of the trade; a legal practice only if the broker first offers the securities publicly at a price higher than the bid.

Cross-border factoring

Concluding a transaction by a network of factors across borders. The exporter's factor can contact correspondent factors in other countries to handle the collection of accounts receivable.

Cross-border risk

Describes the volatility of returns on international investments caused by events associated with a particular country as opposed to events associated solely with a particular economic or financial agent.

Cross-default

A provision under which default on one debt obligation triggers default on another debt obligation.

Cross hedging

Applies to derivative products. Hedging with a futures contract that is different from the underlying being hedged. Use of a hedging instrument different from the security being hedged. Hedging instruments are usually selected to have the highest price correlation to the underlying.

Cross-holdings

The holding by one corporation of shares in another firm. One needs to allow for cross-holdings when aggregating capitalizations of firms. Ignoring cross-holdings leads to double-counting.

Cross rates

The exchange rate between two currencies expressed as the ratio of two foreign exchange rates that are both expressed in terms of a third currency. Foreign exchange rate between two currencies other than the US dollar, the currency in which most exchanges are usually quoted.

Cross-sectional analysis

Assessment of relationships among a cross-section of firms, countries, or some other variable at one particular time.

Cross-Sectional Ratio Analysis

A method of analysis that compares a firm's ratios with some chosen industry benchmark. The benchmark usually chosen is the average ratio value for all firms in an industry for the time period under study.

Cross-sectional approach

A statistical methodology applied to a set of firms at a particular time.

Cross-share holdings

Often used in risk arbitrage. Corporations' or governments' equity share ownership in another corporation's shares.

Cross-border bonds

Bonds that firms issue in the international market.

Crossed market

In the context of general equities, happens when the inside market consists of a highest bid price that is higher than the lowest offer price. See: Overlap the market.

Crossed trade

The prohibited practice of offsetting buy and sell orders without recording the trade on the exchange, thus not allowing other traders to take advantage of a more favorable price.

Crossover rate

The return at which two alternative projects have the same net present value.

Crowd trading

Used for listed equity securities. Group of exchange members with a defined area of function tending to congregate around a trading post pending execution of orders. Includes specialists, floor traders, odd-lot dealers, and other brokers as well as smaller groups with specialized functions. See: Priority.

Crowding out

Heavy federal borrowing that drives interest rates up and prevents businesses and consumers from borrowing when they would like to.

Crown jewel

A particularly profitable or otherwise particularly valuable corporate unit or asset of a firm. Often used in risk arbitrage. The most desirable entities within a diversified corporation as measured by asset value, earning power, and business prospects; in takeover attempts, these entities typically are the main objective of the acquirer and may be sold by a takeover target to make the rest of the company less attractive. See: Scorched earth policy.

CTA

See: Cumulative Translation Adjustment. Also refers to Commodity Trading Advisor.

CU

The two-character ISO 3166 country code for CUBA.

Cum dividend

With dividend; said of a stock whose buyer is eligible to receive a declared dividend. Stocks are usually "cum dividend" for trades made on or before the fifth trading day preceding the record date, when the register of eligible holders is closed for that dividend period. Antithesis of ex-dividend.

Cum rights

With rights.

Cumulative abnormal return (CAR)

Sum of the differences between the expected return on a stock (systematic risk multiplied by the realized market return) and the actual return often used to evaluate the impact of news on a stock price.

Cumulative dividend feature

A requirement that any missed preferred or preference stock dividends be paid in full before any common dividend payment is made.

Cumulative preferred stock

Preferred stock whose dividends accrue, should the issuer not make timely dividend payments. Related: Non-cumulative preferred stock.

Cumulative probability distribution

A function that shows the probability that the random variable will attain a value less than or equal to each value that the random variable can take on.

Cumulative total return

The actual performance of a fund over a particular period.

Cumulative Translation Adjustment (CTA) account

An entry in a translated balance sheet in which gains and/or losses from translation have been accumulated over a period of years. The C.T.A. account is required under the FASB No. 52 rule.

Cumulative voting

A system of voting for directors of a corporation in which shareholder's total number of votes is equal to the number of shares held times the number of candidates.

CUP

The ISO 4217 currency code for Cuban Peso.

The Curb

Another name for the American Stock Exchange (AMEX).

Currency

Money.

Currency appreciation

An increase in the value of one currency relative to another currency. Appreciation occurs when, because of a change in exchange rates, a unit of one currency buys more units of another currency.

Currency arbitrage

Taking advantage of divergences in exchange rates in different money markets by buying a currency in one market and selling it in another market.

Currency basket

The value of a portfolio of specific amounts of individual currencies, used as the basis for setting the market value of another currency. It is also referred to as a currency cocktail.

Currency Board

Entity charged with maintaining the value of a local currency with respect to some other specified currency.

Currency call option

Contract that gives the holder the right to purchase a specific currency at a specified price (exchange rate) within a specific period of time.

Currency depreciation

A decline in the value of one currency relative to another currency. Depreciation occurs when, because of a change in exchange rates, a unit of one currency buys fewer units of another currency.

Currency devaluation

A deliberate downward adjustment in the official exchange rates established, or pegged, by a government against a specified standard, such as another currency or gold.

Currency diversification

Using more than one currency as an investing or financing strategy. Exposure to a diversified currency portfolio typically entails less exchange rate risk than if all the portfolio exposure were in a single foreign currency.

Currency Exchange Risk

Uncertainty about the rate at which revenues or costs denominated in one currency can be converted into another currency.

Currency futures contract

Contract specifying a standard volume of a particular currency to be exchanged on a specific settlement date.

Currency future

A financial future contract for the delivery of a specified foreign currency.

Currency hedge

Applies mainly to international equities. Hedging technique to guard against foreign exchange fluctuations (i.e., short Euro 100 mm when holding a long position of Euro 100 mm in stocks).

Currency in circulation

Paper money, coins, and demand deposits that constitute all the money circulating in the economy.

Currency no longer issued

Old and new series gold and silver certificates, Federal Reserve notes, national bank notes, and 1890 Series Treasury notes.

Currency put option

Contract that gives the holder the right to sell a particular currency at a specified price (exchange rate) within a specified period of time.

Currency option

An option to buy or sell a foreign currency.

Currency overvaluation

Applies mainly to international equities: (1) consideration that a currency is overvalued if private demand for the currency at the going exchange rate is less than total private supply (i.e., central banks are buying up the difference, supporting the value of the currency through foreign exchange intervention); (2) currency value exceeding purchasing power parity.

Currency revaluation

A deliberate upward adjustment in the official exchange rate established, or pegged, by government against a specified standard, such as another currency or gold.

Currency risk

Related: Exchange rate risk.

Currency selection

Asset allocation in which the investor chooses among investments denominated in different currencies.

Currency swap

An agreement to swap a series of specified payment obligations denominated in one currency for a series of specified payment obligations denominated in a different currency.

Current account

Net flow of goods, services, and unilateral transactions (gifts) between countries.

Current account balance

The differnece between the nation's total exports of goods, services and transfer and its total imports of them. Current account balance calculations exclude transactions in financial assets and liabilities.

Current assets

Value of cash, accounts receivable, inventories, marketable securities and other assets that could be converted to cash in less than 1 year.

Current coupon

A bond selling at or close to par, that is, a bond with a coupon close to the yields currently offered on new bonds of a similar maturity and credit risk.

Current Coupon Bond

Bonds on which the coupon is set approximately equal to the bonds' yield to maturity at the time of their issuance.

Current-coupon issues

Related: Benchmark issues.

Current Dollars

The actual dollar amount paid in sales transactions.

Current income

Money that is routinely received from investments in the form of dividends, interest, and other income sources.

Current income bonds

Bonds paying semiannual interest to holders. Interest is not included in the accrued discount.

Current issue

In Treasury securities, the most recently auctioned issue. Trading is more active in current issues than in off-the-run issues.

Current liabilities

Amount owed for salaries, interest, accounts payable and other debts due within 1 year.

Current market value

The value of a client's portfolio at today's market price, as listed in a brokerage statement.

Current maturity

Current time to maturity on an outstanding debt instrument.

Current/noncurrent method

The translation of all of a foreign subsidiary's current assets and liabilities into home currency at the current exchange rate while noncurrent assets and liabilities are translated at the historical exchange rate; that is, the rate in effect at the time the asset was acquired or the liability incurred.

Current production rate

The highest interest rate permissible on current Government National Mortgage Association, mortgage-backed securities.

Current rate method

The translation of all foreign currency balance sheet and income statement items at the current exchange rate.

Current ratio

Indicator of short-term debt-paying ability. Determined by dividing current assets by current liabilities. The higher the ratio, the more liquid the company.

Currency risk sharing

An agreement by the parties to a transaction to share the currency risk associated with the transaction. The arrangement involves a customized hedge contract embedded in the underlying transaction.

Current yield

For bonds or notes, the coupon rate divided by the market price of the bond.

Cushion

The minimum period between the time a bond is issued and the time it is called.

Cushion bonds

High-coupon bonds that sell at only at a moderate premium because they are callable at a price below that at which a comparable noncallable bond would sell. Cushion bonds offer considerable downside protection in a falling market.

Cushion theory

The theory that a stock with many short positions taken in it will rise, because these positions must be covered by the stock.

CUSIP

See: Committee on Uniform Securities Identification Procedures.

CUSIP number

Unique number given to a security to distinguish it from other stocks and registered bonds. See: Committee on Uniform Securities Identification Procedures.

Custodial fees

Fees charged by an institution that holds securities in safekeeping for an investor.

Custodian

Either (1) a bank, agent, trust company, or other organization responsible for safeguarding financial assets, or (2) the individual who oversees the mutual fund assets of a minor's custodial account.

Custodian bank

Applies mainly to international equities. Bank or other financial institution that keeps custody of stock certificates and other assets of a mutual fund, individual, or corporate client. See: Depository Trust Company (DTC)

Customary payout ratios

A range of payout ratios that is typical according to an analysis of comparable firms.

"Customer picking prices"

Customer is firm on price and has set the price at which to transact.

Customer's loan consent

Agreement signed by a margin customer that allows a broker to borrow margined securities up to the level of the customer's debit balance to help cover other customers' short positions.

Customers' net debit balance

The total amount of credit given by NYSE member firms to finance customers purchasing securities.

Customized benchmarks

A benchmark that is designed to meet a client's requirements and long-term objectives.

Customs Broker

An individual or firm licensed by customs authorities to enter and clear imported goods through customs. The broker represents the importer in dealings with the customs authorities.

Customized Sales Survey

The CSS is a fee-based International Trade Administration service that provides firms with key marketing, pricing, and foreign representation information about their specific products. Overseas staff conduct on-site interviews to provide data in nine marketing areas about the product, such as sales potential in the market, comparable products, distribution channels, going price, competitive factors, and qualified purchasers. Additional information may be provided to clients at additional charge. This product was formerly known as the Comparison Shopping Service.

Customs

The authorities designated to collect duties levied by a country on imports and exports. The term also applies to the procedures involved in such collection.

Customs Broker - Customhouse Broker

Licensed by U.S. Customs to clear shipments for clients, also can forward goods "In Bond" to y our port.

Customs Cooperation Council

The CCC is an international organization consisting of representatives of about 150 countries. The Council serve as a technical body which studies and seeks to resolve the various countries' customs problems in an attempt to harmonize customs operations and promote trade. The Council was established in 1950; headquarters are in Brussels, Belgium.

Customs Cooperation Council Nomenclature

A customs tariff nomenclature formerly used by many countries, including most European nations but not the United States. It has been superseded by the Harmonized System Nomenclature to which most major trading nations, including the U.S., adhere.

Customs Electronic Bulletin Board

The CEEB provides information on rulings, quotas, currency conversion rates, customs valuation provisions, directives, and other customs news. The CEBB is available without charge, 7 days each week at 202-376-7100 (9600 baud) with PC communication switches set to no parity, 8 bit words and 1 stop bit. Voice information may be obtained by calling 202-376-7039.

Customs Free Zone

See: Free Trade Zone.

Customshouse Broker

The U.S. Customs Service defines a CHB, or Customs Broker, as any person who is licensed in accordance with Part III of Title 19 of the Code of Federal Regulations (Customs regulations) to transact Customs business on behalf of others. Customs business is limited to those activities involving transactions with Customs concerning the entry and admissibility of merchandise; its classification and valuation; the payment of duties, taxes, or other charges assessed or collected by Customs upon merchandise by reason of its importation, or the refund, rebate, or drawback thereof. (See 19 CFR 111.1(b) and (c).)

Customs Import Value

This is the U.S. Customs Service appraisal value of merchandise. Methodologically, the Customs value is similar to f.a.s. (free alongside ship) value since it is based on the value of the product in the foreign country of origin, and excludes charges incurred in bringing the merchandise to the United States (import duties, ocean freight, insurance, and so forth); but it differs in that the U.S. Customs Service, not the importer or exporter, has the final authority to determine the value of the good.

Customs Union

An agreement between two or more countries to remove trade barriers with each other and to establish common tariff and nontariff policies with respect to imports from countries outside of the agreement. The European Community is the most well-known example. The two primary trade effects of a customs union are: (a) trade creation — the shift from consumption of domestic production toward consumption of member imports and (b) trade diversion — the shift from trade with non-member countries in favor of trade with member countries.

Cut Off Date

The date prescribed in the unclaimed property law in most states for determining the items of property that must be turned over to the state. See: Escheat.

Cutoff point

The lowest rate of return acceptable on investments.

CV

The two-character ISO 3166 country code for CAPE VERDE.

CVE

The ISO 4217 currency code for Cape Verde Islands Escudo.

CX

The two-character ISO 3166 country code for CHRISTMAS ISLAND.

CY

The two-character ISO 3166 country code for CYPRUS.

Cycles

A full orbital period.

Cyclical stock

Stock that tends to rise quickly when the economy turns up and fall quickly when the economy turns down. Examples are housing, automobiles, and paper.

Cyclical unemployment

Unemployment caused by a low level of aggregate demand associated with recession in the business cycle.

CYP

The ISO 4217 currency code for Cyprus Pound.

CZ

The two-character ISO 3166 country code for CZECH REPUBLIC.

CZK

The ISO 4217 currency code for Czech Republic Koruna.